THE HISTORY & CULTURE of NATIVE AMERICANS

The Mohawk

THE HISTORY & CULTURE of NATIVE AMERICANS

The Apache

The Blackfeet

The Cherokee

The Cheyenne

The Choctaw

The Comanche

The Hopi

The Iroquois

The Lakota Sioux

The Mohawk

The Nez Perce

The Navajo

The Seminole

The Zuni

THE HISTORY & CULTURE of NATIVE AMERICANS

The Mohawk

SAMUEL WILLARD CROMPTON

Series Editor
PAUL C. ROSIER

CHELSEA HOUSE
PUBLISHERS
An imprint of Infobase Publishing

The Mohawk

Copyright © 2010 by Infobase Publishing

Chelsea House
An imprint of Infobase Publishing
132 West 31st Street
New York NY 10001

Library of Congress Cataloging-in-Publication Data

Crompton, Samuel Willard.
   The Mohawk / By Samuel Willard Crompton.
     p. cm. — (The history and culture of native Americans)
   Includes bibliographical references and index.
   ISBN 978-1-60413-787-3 (hardcover)
   1. Mohawk Indians—History—Juvenile literature. I. Title. II. Series.

   E99.M8C627   2010
   974.7004'975542—dc22   2010012036

Text design by Lina Farinella
Cover design by Alicia Post
Composition by Newgen
Cover printed by Bang Printing, Brainerd, MN
Book printed and bound by Bang Printing, Brainerd, MN
Date printed: September 2010
Printed in the United States of America

10 9 8 7 6 5 4 3 2 1
This book is printed on acid-free paper.

Contents

Foreword
by Paul C. Rosier

Native American words, phrases, and tribal names are embedded in the very geography of the United States—in the names of creeks, rivers, lakes, cities, and states, including Alabama, Connecticut, Iowa, Kansas, Illinois, Missouri, Oklahoma, and many others. Yet Native Americans remain the most misunderstood ethnic group in the United States. This is a result of limited coverage of Native American history in middle schools, high schools, and colleges; poor coverage of contemporary Native American issues in the news media; and stereotypes created by Hollywood movies, sporting events, and TV shows.

Two newspaper articles about American Indians caught my eye in recent months. Paired together, they provide us with a good introduction to the experiences of American Indians today: first, how they are stereotyped and turned into commodities; and second, how they see themselves being a part of the United States and of the wider world. (Note: I use the terms *Native Americans* and *American Indians* interchangeably; both terms are considered appropriate.)

In the first article, "Humorous Souvenirs to Some, Offensive Stereotypes to Others," written by Carol Berry in *Indian Country Today,* I read that tourist shops in Colorado were selling "souvenir" T-shirts portraying American Indians as drunks. "My Indian name is Runs with Beer," read one T-shirt offered in Denver. According to the article, the T-shirts are "the kind of stereotype-reinforcing products also seen in nearby Boulder, Estes Park, and likely other Colorado communities, whether as part of the tourism trade or as everyday merchandise." No other ethnic group in the United States is stereotyped in such a public fashion. In addition, Native people are used to sell a range of consumer goods, including the Jeep Cherokee, Red Man chewing tobacco, Land O'Lakes butter, and other items that either objectify or insult them, such as cigar store Indians. As importantly, non-Indians learn about American Indian history and culture through sports teams such as the Atlanta Braves, Cleveland Indians, Florida State Seminoles, or Washington Redskins, whose name many American Indians consider a racist insult; dictionaries define *redskin* as a "disparaging" or "offensive" term for American Indians. When fans in Atlanta do their "tomahawk chant" at Braves baseball games, they perform two inappropriate and related acts: One, they perpetuate a stereotype of American Indians as violent; and two, they tell a historical narrative that covers up the violent ways that Georgians treated the Cherokee during the Removal period of the 1830s.

The second article, written by Melissa Pinion-Whitt of the San Bernardino *Sun,* addressed an important but unknown dimension of Native American societies that runs counter to the irresponsible and violent image created by products and sporting events. The article, "San Manuels Donate $1.7 M for Aid to Haiti," described a Native American community that had sent aid to Haiti after it was devastated in January 2010 by an earthquake that killed more than 200,000 people, injured hundreds of thousands more, and destroyed the Haitian capital. The San Manuel Band of Mission Indians in California donated $1.7 million to help relief efforts in Haiti; San Manuel children held fund-raisers to collect additional donations. For the San Manuel Indians it was nothing new; in 2007 they had donated $1 million to help Sudanese refugees in Darfur. San Manuel also contributed $700,000 to relief efforts following Hurricane Katrina and Hurricane Rita, and donated $1 million in 2007 for wildfire recovery in Southern California.

Such generosity is consistent with many American Indian nations' cultural practices, such as the "give-away," in which wealthy tribal members give to the needy, and the "potlatch," a winter gift-giving ceremony and feast tradition shared by tribes in the Pacific Northwest. And it is consistent with historical accounts of American Indians' generosity. For example, in 1847 Cherokee and Choctaw, who had recently survived their forced march on a "Trail of Tears" from their homelands in the American South to present-day Oklahoma, sent aid to Irish families after reading of the potato famine, which created a similar forced migration of Irish. A Cherokee newspaper editorial, quoted in Christine Kinealy's *The Great Irish Famine: Impact, Ideology, and Rebellion,* explained that the Cherokee "will be richly repaid by the consciousness of having done a good act, by the moral effect it will produce abroad." During and after World War II, nine Pueblo communities in New Mexico offered to donate food to the hungry in Europe, after Pueblo army veterans told stories of suffering they had witnessed while serving in the United States armed forces overseas. Considering themselves a part of the wider world, Native people have reached beyond their borders, despite their own material poverty, to help create a peaceful world community.

American Indian nations have demonstrated such generosity within the United States, especially in recent years. After the terrorist attacks of September 11, 2001, the Lakota Sioux in South Dakota offered police officers and emergency medical personnel to New York City to help with relief efforts; Indian nations across the country sent millions of dollars to help the victims of the attacks. As an editorial in the *Native American Times* newspaper explained on September 12, 2001, "American Indians love this country like no other. . . . Today, we are all New Yorkers."

Indeed, Native Americans have sacrificed their lives in defending the United States from its enemies in order to maintain their right to be both American and Indian. As the volumes in this series tell us, Native Americans patriotically served as soldiers (including as "code talkers") during World War I and World War II, as well as during the Korean War, the Vietnam War, and, after 9/11, the wars in Afghanistan and Iraq. Native soldiers, men and women, do so today by the tens of thousands because they believe in America, an

America that celebrates different cultures and peoples. Sgt. Leonard Gouge, a Muscogee Creek, explained it best in an article in *Cherokee News Path* in discussing his post-9/11 army service. He said he was willing to serve his country abroad because "by supporting the American way of life, I am preserving the Indian way of life."

This new Chelsea House series has two main goals. The first is to document the rich diversity of American Indian societies and the ways their cultural practices and traditions have evolved over time. The second goal is to provide the reader with coverage of the complex relationships that have developed between non-Indians and Indians over the past several hundred years. This history helps to explain why American Indians consider themselves both American and Indian and why they see preserving this identity as a strength of the American way of life, as evidence to the rest of the world that America is a champion of cultural diversity and religious freedom. By exploring Native Americans' cultural diversity and their contributions to the making of the United States, these volumes confront the stereotypes that paint all American Indians as the same and portray them as violent; as "drunks," as those Colorado T-shirts do; or as rich casino owners, as many news accounts do.

* * *

Each of the 14 volumes in this series is written by a scholar who shares my conviction that young adult readers are both fascinated by Native American history and culture and have not been provided with sufficient material to properly understand the diverse nature of this complex history and culture. The authors themselves represent a varied group that includes university teachers and professional writers, men and women, and Native and non-Native. To tell these fascinating stories, this talented group of scholars has examined an incredible variety of sources, both the primary sources that historical actors have created and the secondary sources that historians and anthropologists have written to make sense of the past.

Although the 14 Indian nations (also called tribes and communities) selected for this series have different histories and cultures, they all share certain common experiences. In particular, they had to face an American empire that spread westward in the eighteenth and nineteenth centuries, causing great trauma and change for all Native people in the process. Because each volume documents American Indians' experiences dealing with powerful non-Indian institutions and ideas, I outline below the major periods and features of federal Indian policy-making in order to provide a frame of reference for complex processes of change with which American Indians had to contend. These periods—Assimilation, Indian New Deal, Termination, Red Power, and Self-determination—and specific acts of legislation that define them—in particular the General Allotment Act, the Indian Reorganization Act, and the Indian Self-determination and Education Assistance Act—will appear in all the volumes, especially in the latter chapters.

In 1851, the commissioner of the federal Bureau of Indian Affairs (BIA) outlined a three-part program for subduing American Indians militarily and assimilating them into the United States: concentration, domestication, and incorporation. In the first phase, the federal government waged war with the American Indian nations of the American West in order to "concentrate" them on reservations, away from expanding settlements of white Americans and immigrants. Some American Indian nations experienced terrible violence in resisting federal troops and state militia; others submitted peacefully and accepted life on a reservation. During this phase, roughly from the 1850s to the 1880s, the U.S. government signed hundreds of treaties with defeated American Indian nations. These treaties "reserved" to these American Indian nations specific territory as well as the use of natural resources. And they provided funding for the next phase of "domestication."

During the domestication phase, roughly the 1870s to the early 1900s, federal officials sought to remake American Indians in the mold of white Americans. Through the Civilization Program, which actually started with President Thomas Jefferson, federal officials sent religious missionaries, farm instructors, and teachers to the newly created reservations in an effort to "kill the Indian to save the man," to use a phrase of that time. The ultimate goal was to extinguish American Indian cultural traditions and turn American Indians into Christian yeoman farmers. The most important piece of legislation in this period was the General Allotment Act (or Dawes Act), which mandated that American Indian nations sell much of their territory to white farmers and use the proceeds to farm on what was left of their homelands. The program was a failure, for the most part, because white farmers got much of the best arable land in the process. Another important part of the domestication agenda was the federal boarding school program, which required all American Indian children to attend schools to further their rejection of Indian ways and the adoption of non-Indian ways. The goal of federal reformers, in sum, was to incorporate (or assimilate) American Indians into American society as individual citizens and not as groups with special traditions and religious practices.

During the 1930s some federal officials came to believe that American Indians deserved the right to practice their own religion and sustain their identity as Indians, arguing that such diversity made America stronger. During the Indian New Deal period of the 1930s, BIA commissioner John Collier devised the Indian Reorganization Act (IRA), which passed in 1934, to give American Indian nations more power, not less. Not all American Indians supported the IRA, but most did. They were eager to improve their reservations, which suffered from tremendous poverty that resulted in large measure from federal policies such as the General Allotment Act.

Some federal officials opposed the IRA, however, and pushed for the assimilation of American Indians in a movement called Termination. The two main goals of Termination advocates, during the 1950s and 1960s, were to end (terminate) the federal reservation system and American Indians' political sovereignty derived from treaties and to relocate American Indians from rural reservations to urban areas. These coercive federal assimilation policies in turn generated resistance from Native Americans, including young activists who helped to create the so-called Red Power era of the 1960s and 1970s, which coincided with the African-American civil rights movement. This resistance led to the federal government's rejection of Termination policies in 1970. And in 1975 the U.S. Congress passed the Indian Self-determination and Education Assistance Act, which made it the government's policy to support American Indians' right to determine the future of their communities. Congress then passed legislation to help American Indian nations to improve reservation life; these acts strengthened American Indians' religious freedom, political sovereignty, and economic opportunity.

All American Indians, especially those in the western United States, were affected in some way by the various federal policies described above. But it is important to highlight the fact that each American Indian community responded in different ways to these pressures for change, both the detribalization policies of assimilation and the retribalization policies of self-determination. There is no one group of "Indians." American Indians were and still are a very diverse group. Some embraced the assimilation programs of the federal government and rejected the old traditions; others refused to adopt non-Indian customs or did so selectively, on their own terms. Most American Indians, as I noted above, maintain a dual identity of American and Indian.

Today, there are more than 550 American Indian (and Alaska Natives) nations recognized by the federal government. They have a legal and political status similar to states, but they have special rights and privileges that are the result of congressional acts and the hundreds of treaties that still govern federal-Indian relations today. In July 2008, the total population of American Indians (and Alaska Natives) was 4.9 million, representing about 1.6 percent of the United States population. The state with the highest number of American Indians is California, followed by Oklahoma, home to the Cherokee (the largest American Indian nation in terms of population), and then Arizona, home to the Navajo (the second-largest American Indian nation). All told, roughly half of the American Indian population lives in urban areas; the other half lives on reservations and in other rural parts of the country. Like all their fellow American citizens, American Indians pay federal taxes, obey federal laws, and vote in federal, state, and local elections; they also participate in the democratic processes of their American Indian nations, electing judges, politicians, and other civic officials.

This series on the history and culture of Native Americans celebrates their diversity and differences as well as the ways they have strengthened the broader community of America. Ronnie Lupe, the chairman of the White Mountain Apache government in Arizona, once addressed questions from non-Indians as to "why Indians serve the United States with such distinction and honor?" Lupe, a Korean War veteran, answered those questions during the Gulf War of 1991–1992, in which Native American soldiers served to protect the independence of the Kuwaiti people. He explained in "Chairman's Corner" in *The Fort Apache Scout* that "our loyalty to the United States goes beyond our need to defend our home and reservation lands. . . . Only a few in this country really understand that the indigenous people are a national treasure. Our values have the potential of creating the social, environmental, and spiritual healing that could make this country truly great."

—Paul C. Rosier
Associate Professor of History
Villanova University

Northeast Woodland Peoples

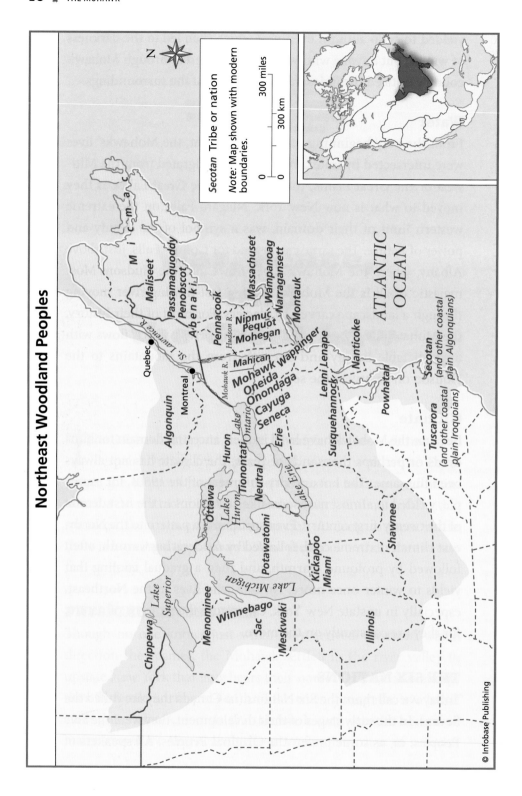

Secotan Tribe or nation

Note: Map shown with modern boundaries.

300 miles

300 km

0

0

ATLANTIC OCEAN

Mi'cmac

Maliseet

Passamaquoddy

Penobscot

Abenaki

Pennacook

Massachuset

Wampanoag

Narragansett

Montauk

Nipmuc

Pequot

Mohegan

Quebec

St. Lawrence R.

Hudson R.

Mahican

Mohawk Wappinger

Oneida

Onondaga

Cayuga

Seneca

Nanticoke

Lenni Lenape

Susquehannock

Powhatan

Secotan (and other coastal plain Algonquians)

Tuscarora (and other coastal plain Iroquoians)

Montreal

Mohawk R.

Algonquin

Ottawa

Huron

Tionontati

Neutral

Lake Huron

Lake Ontario

Lake Erie

Erie

Potawatomi

Menominee

Winnebago

Sac

Meskwaki

Kickapoo

Miami

Illinois

Shawnee

Lake Michigan

Chippewa

Lake Superior

© Infobase Publishing

the Iroquois language, they came to dominate upstate New York, and divided its landscape among the five tribes. The Mohawk, also called the "people of the flint," were known as the keepers of the eastern door of the "Iroquois Longhouse," because they faced toward the Hudson River and the Algonquian-speaking peoples such as the Mohican (or Mahican). Next, from east to west, came the Oneida, the "people of the great stone," who occupied the lands and waters just west of the Mohawk. The two tribes saw each other as brothers, with the Mohawk generally perceived as the elder. Just to their west were the Onondaga, the largest of the Five Peoples. The great council fire of the Five Nations burned continually at their principal town. West of them were the Cayuga, who lived in the Finger Lakes region, and to their west were the Seneca, whose lands ended at the mighty horse-shoe falls known as Niagara.

WAR

Nearly all Mohawk and Iroquois legends speak of a dark and dangerous time, many centuries past, when the Five Peoples fought each other and their neighbors nonstop. Why they did this is uncertain, for the lands of New York provided abundance for all. But the sad truth is that the Five Peoples fought each other with increasing ferocity, and, sometime during the darkness, they engaged in the practice of cannibalism. (Some anthropologists point to the American Indian belief that by eating the heart of an enemy, one could gain his *Manitou,* or spirit, for oneself.) Virtually all oral traditions concur that this dark time came to an end when

(Opposite map) The Northeast Woodland tribes were forest dwellers that inhabited a wide area of the eastern United States, including present-day New England, the Canadian Maritimes, the Great Lakes Region, the Mid-Atlantic states, and the Midwest. There were many tribes, including those that made up the great Iroquois Confederacy (Mohawk, Oneida, Onondaga, Cayuga, and Seneca). The Tuscarora would later join the confederacy.

the "Master of Life" chose an outsider to bring the Great Law of Peace to the Five Peoples. That outsider was Deganawidah.

DEGANAWIDAH

He was a member of the Huron, an Algonquian-speaking tribe that lived on the western side of the Handsome Lake. Whether in a dream or a direct vision, Deganawidah had a visit from the Master of Life, as the being was called by many of the Northeast Woodland peoples. ("Great Spirit" was the expression used in the American West.) This supreme being told Deganawidah to cross the Handsome Lake (now known as Lake Ontario) and to convert the Five Peoples to the Great Law of Peace, whose conditions he named. There was one very significant problem: Deganawidah had a bad stammer.

The Five Peoples (and later the Five Nations) had a great respect, even worship, for the spoken word. A man who was good with words was esteemed as much as one who was proficient with a bow and arrow. Very likely, the Five Peoples would not listen to a man with a speech impediment. Knowing this, Deganawidah asked the Master of Life to be released from his task, but the supreme being insisted. Perhaps the moral to be drawn from this story is that one's life task seldom comes easily. Rather, one is intended to struggle in order to become a fuller human being.

According to tradition, Deganawidah crossed the Handsome Lake in a canoe made of white stone. This sounds ridiculous to modern ears, but to the Five Peoples of his time it symbolized that one should undertake the most difficult task first, and surely there was no harder task than traveling in a stone canoe. (The color white symbolized purity of intention.) Reaching the eastern side of the Handsome Lake, Deganawidah began a series of journeys that took him from present-day Buffalo to present-day Albany, and many places in between. Everywhere he went, he spoke— haltingly—of the Master of Life's distress with the Five Peoples, and his desire that they come to live together in one symbolic longhouse, under the shelter of the Great Tree of Peace. A few people listened, but most rejected the foreigner whose tongue was so trippingly tied.

The Mohawk have many stories of Deganawidah, who, they say, spent more time with them than any of the other four tribes. A wonderful tale has Deganawidah being swept over the 80-foot (24-meter) drop at Cohoes Falls, to be rescued by a floating branch at the last second. This symbolism likely speaks to the rush (of words and water) and the need to keep one's balance while engaged in the great task assigned by the Master of Life.

No matter whether the Mohawk tales are literally true, or whether they have been embellished with the passage of time, virtually all Iroquois agree that Deganawidah spent many years at the task. He considered himself a complete failure until one day he saw the back of an Onondaga warrior and heard the sound of tears coming from him. Hiawatha was a great fighter who had participated in bloodshed, but all the thrill of these activities was swept out of him when his wife and three children were killed in a raid. We do not know which stream received his tears that day, only that as he wept bitterly, Hiawatha looked into the water to see the figure of a man behind him. Leaping to his feet and turning round, Hiawatha prepared for battle, but one look into the warm eyes and luminous face of Deganawidah persuaded him that there was no danger.

In a matter of minutes, the hardened heart of Hiawatha was opened, and he experienced the healing power of mercy. Years seemed to drop away, and he felt the joy of life, even though he could not forget its pain. There, in that encounter, was born the condolence ceremony. This became—and remained—a vital ritual of the Mohawk and their fellow four nations. Every significant meeting, encounter, or council fire began with a condolence ceremony, in which the leaders of one tribe or clan would symbolically wipe the tears from the eyes of their peers, open their ears that they might hear correctly, and remove the clots or blocks in the chest and throat so they might feel and speak properly.

ATOTARHO

Deganawidah and Hiawatha became an inseparable duo, spreading the news of the Great Law of Peace through the lands of the Five Peoples. Hiawatha was a formidable speaker, and his oratory—joined with the luminous presence of Deganawidah—conspired to make them successful with most clans, tribes, and persons. There were holdouts, however, the most formidable of whom was Atotarho (or Addaharho).

An Onondaga warrior, Atotarho was also an accomplished sorcerer. To show his kinship with the powers of nature, he had twisted his hair into the shape of snakes, and many opponents shrank from any sort of encounter. Deganawidah and Hiawatha found it impossible to confront Atotarho directly. His magic was too strong. Only by finding allies among other Onondaga were they able to show this powerful sorcerer the error of his ways. Even then, Atotarho demanded a price for his agreement: the central village of the Onondaga people (in present-day Syracuse, New York) must be the location for all council fires, for all time. Moreover, the Onondaga must have 14 elected sachems to attend the council fire, unlike the Mohawk, who had 9.

Deganawidah and Hiawatha agreed to the wily man's terms. They then proceeded to comb the snakes out of his hair, and to announce that Atotarho was now a civilized being, a member of one of the Five Nations, which replaced the Five Peoples. Though some historians and anthropologists view Atotarho as a throwback to earlier, more violent times, or as an obstructionist, to the Mohawk mind he is a folk hero, able to withstand even the sweet smiles of Deganawidah and the brilliant speeches of Hiawatha. Atotarho came to embody superhuman traits and his name was used after his death as a symbol of glory and honor among the Onondaga. From his insistence, the concept of the central council fire was born, and the fire at Onondaga would remain lit (symbolically) for hundreds of years.

Who knows which is more difficult: to cross a lake in a stone canoe, to preach the Great Law of Peace from a damaged set of

Atotarho (or Tadodaho) became one of the most influential chiefs in New York State. He had matted snakelike hair, and he could supposedly kill his enemies from a distance without even seeing them. This illustration, made in the 1850s by U.S. Army captain Seth Eastman, shows Atotarho receiving spokesmen Hiawatha and Deganawidah.

vocal cords, or to comb snakes from a sorcerer's hair? All one can say for certain is that Deganawidah had indeed accomplished everything that the Master of Life required.

MODERN RESEARCH

For generations, scholars have attempted to date the founding of the Iroquois Longhouse. When the first European settlers asked the Five Nations, they received the reply that it was many generations ago. Over time, however, a scholarly consensus built that it was sometime in the sixteenth century, with able historians looking to the pattern of solar eclipses to strengthen their arguments.

(According to tradition, the final agreement to the Great Law of Peace took place under a darkened sky.) Some spoke of the year 1570, while others argued for 1536. In 1998, Barbara C. Mann and Jerry L. Fields, both of the University of Toledo, came up with something much earlier and more specific: August 31, 1142. That would place the founding of the Five Nations Confederacy in the High Middle Ages of medieval Europe. If accurate, it means that the Five Nations are much older than was previously believed, and that the Five Nations Confederacy was an organized body for longer than England's House of Commons, which developed in the thirteenth century.

Mann and Fields built a series of careful arguments for the specific date. They examined the pattern of solar eclipses in the upstate New York area, and found that several would not have darkened the sky in the area around Syracuse. They found one that occurred on August 31, 1142, but that was not enough to satisfy their intellectual curiosity. Mann and Fields went further, analyzing the lifetimes and years of rule of major political and religious figures, such as U.S. presidents, British prime ministers, and Roman Catholic popes. Arriving at an average span of time in power, Mann and Fields multiplied the average period of governing control by the number of Onondaga sachems (chiefs) who had held the title Atotarho. They came up with a year sometime around A.D. 1150, close enough to the 1142 date to give them reasonable assurance. Based on their careful work, many scholars now agree that the Five Peoples became the Five Nations in the period Europeans call the High Middle Ages, and that something like 21 generations of Mohawk, Oneida, Onondaga, Cayuga, and Seneca were born before the arrival of Europeans in the early seventeenth century.

THE GREAT LAW

Certainly, one can imagine that another scholar will one day use similar evidence to come up with another date for the founding of the Five Nations, but it seems likely that most revisionist history will still point to an earlier date for the founding, not a later one. This puts a very different look on Iroquoian studies, for one realizes that the peoples who met Henry Hudson and Samuel de Champlain had been organized, politically and culturally, for a very long time.

The lands of upstate New York were much the same in 1609 as they had been in 1142. The abundant soil produced a rich type of corn that would make the Mohawk famous. The waters had neither altered their courses, nor the strength with which they flowed. The great falls at Niagara still sent millions of gallons spilling every minute, and the smaller waterfalls at Cohoes continued to mark a boundary between the Mohawk and their Algonquian-speaking neighbors.

The climate conditions were different, though. If the date of 1142 is accurate, then the Five Peoples became the Five Nations toward the end of the long warming spell that had sent the Vikings out from Scandinavia, and which had greatly increased the crop yields of medieval Europe. The great warming ended in the late thirteenth century, and by the time the Mohawk met their first Europeans, North America and Western Europe were both locked into the early stages of what climatologists call the Little Ice Age.

Perhaps it is fitting, symbolically, that the Iroquois Confederacy was founded during a time of climate warming. Certainly, the descendants of Deganawidah, Hiawatha, and Atotarho would experience a major change, both in the climate and their relationship to neighbors: namely, the Europeans, who began to arrive in 1609.

Black Robes and White Priests

One of the earliest and best descriptions of the Five Nations comes from the pen of a Frenchman writing in 1666:

> The Iroquois nation consists of nine tribes which form two divisions; one of four tribes and the other of five.
>
> They call the first division *Guey-niotiteshesgue,* which means the four tribes; and the second division they call it *Ouiche-niotiteteshgue,* which means the five tribes.
>
> The first is that of the tortoise, which calls itself *Atiniathin.* It is the first, because they pretend, when the Master of Life made the earth, that he placed it on a tortoise; and when there are earthquakes, it is the tortoise that stirs.

The author, whose work is recorded in the first volume of the *Documentary History of the State of New York,* published in 1849, clearly made some errors, but he was on the right track.

The Five Nations were separated into clans, designed around the totem of certain animals. The tortoise clan was important, but so were those of the bear and the wolf. Later, because of a booming fur trade with the Europeans, another clan would be designed around the beaver. Thanks to the tireless research of Barbara J. Sivertsen, published as *Turtles, Wolves, and Bears: A Mohawk Family History,* we now know a great deal more about the separate lineages within the Mohawk Nation. One thing that comes to the forefront time and again is the importance to the Mohawk of clan continuity. They were a traditionally minded people who named their sachems for the original ones, those who had lived in the time of Deganawidah and Hiawatha.

The Mohawk were the first of the Five Nations to encounter Europeans.

THE FRENCH

In the summer of 1608, Samuel de Champlain established the first permanent European settlement at what is now Quebec City in Quebec, Canada. One year later, he and two other French colonists accompanied a war party of Montagnais who were headed south to fight their traditional foes, the Mohawk. Champlain knew little to nothing about the Mohawk; his intention was to make a firm alliance with the Montagnais. Sometime in July (the date remains in dispute), Champlain and the Montagnais met a Mohawk war party on the west bank of what is now called Lake Champlain in his honor.

The battle was short. The Mohawk and Montagnais lined up, brandished war clubs and bows and arrows, and were about to clash, when the Montagnais parted ranks to allow Champlain to come forward. He planted his harquebus (an early form of musket) on a tripod and fired shots that killed two or three of the Mohawk chiefs. The Mohawk, who had never seen (much less *heard*) a European gun before, were put to flight, with the Montagnais pursuing and killing many. Champlain naturally saw this as a signal victory, in which European firearms played a decisive role. He did

This engraving depicts the battle between the Iroquois and Samuel de Champlain and his allies, the Algonquian, in 1609. The illustration is based on a drawing by Champlain.

not realize, however, that he had made ardent foes of the Mohawk, or that they would nearly destroy his fledgling colony in a series of wars.

THE DUTCH

It is a coincidence—an interesting one to be sure—that other European people came the same year as the battle on the shores of Lake Champlain. In September 1609, about five weeks after the battle, Henry Hudson (an Englishman in the service of Holland) sailed the *Half Moon* past what is now New York City. Hudson perceived the great potential of Manhattan Island, but he sailed on, up the river that now bears his name, until he reached the area of what is now Albany. There he anchored and remained for two weeks, during which time the nearby Mohawk learned of his presence. Hudson did not record meeting any Mohawk (the record suggests that he met the Mohican instead), but this second meeting between whites and Natives in New York was full of omens for the future.

THE FOUR TOWNS

Over the next generation, the Mohawk and the other members of the Five Nations became familiar with the French and the Dutch, who settled at Quebec and Montreal in Canada, and at Albany and Manhattan in New York. The Iroquois were not pleased with these invasions of their traditional homelands (they claimed the St. Lawrence and Mohawk rivers) but the Europeans had items they desired: guns, gunpowder, iron kettles, and iron axes.

To the best of our knowledge, most Native Americans were interested in muskets and rifles. To people who had hunted with bows, arrows, and rocks, the appearance of the musket (and later the rifle) was an amazing thing. These European-made instruments were more accurate and deadly than the weapons used by American Indians at the time. A tradition of dependency on European goods was thus established, with French and Dutch trading posts set up near Mohawk territory.

Iron and copper instruments were valued almost as much as muskets and gunpowder, for the Mohawk had nothing like these in their traditional stock of tools. In order to obtain all the things they desired, the Mohawk had to bring something of value to the Europeans. Luckily, they had one thing in great abundance: beaver furs. Anyone who has ever worn a beaver hat or cloak during a severe winter can appreciate the wonderful warmth it provides, and the French and Dutch arrived in North America just in time for one of the coldest periods of the Little Ice Age, which lasted off

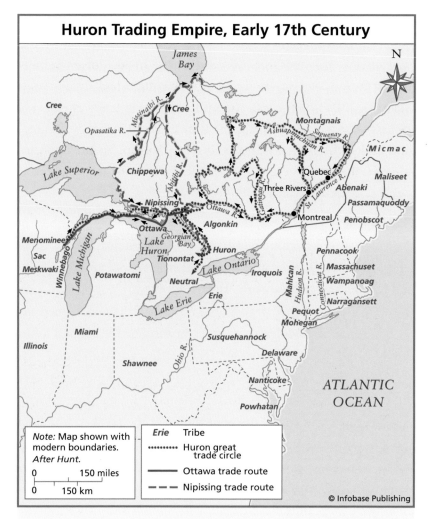

Huron Trading Empire, Early 17th Century

As the map indicates, the Huron were the first masters of the fur trade, bringing beaver pelts from the Great Lakes and Hudson's Bay to Montreal. The Five Nations of Iroquois struck at the Huron in the 1640s, practically eliminating the tribe, and opening the way for Iroquois mastery of the trade, centered on Albany, New York.

and on from about 1300 until about 1850. Little wonder, then, that beaver fur was in high demand.

The Mohawk brought their pelts to Albany or Montreal, depending on which European people paid a higher price. Over time, the Mohawk became dependent on the firearms and equipment of the Europeans. Little difference was made when the English replaced the Dutch in 1664 as the major power brokers in Albany and Manhattan; the economic pattern had already been established. By about 1650, the Mohawk had entirely tapped out the beaver supply in their region. They engaged in a series of conflicts called the Beaver Wars against the Huron, on the opposite side of Lake Ontario, and against the River Indians, with whom they had previously been friendly.

No one who knows Mohawk history would claim that they were a peace-loving people before the Europeans arrived, but the competition for beaver furs and the economic rewards made their warfare even more damaging. By about 1660, the Mohawk had virtually destroyed the Huron Nation. Ironically, Deganawidah, the man who had spread the Great Law of Peace, had been Huron.

The wars with the Huron and other tribes brought the Mohawk into continued conflict with the French-Canadian colony, and there were decades during which the lands between the two peoples were filled with raiding parties. The Mohawk won many, if not most, of the encounters because of their skill in wilderness warfare. Even so, there were days, and even months, of peace in which peoples migrated back and forth. A number of Iroquois sometimes showed up at Quebec City, saying that their dreams had led them to make the journey. (Dreams were an important part of Five Nations culture.)

The Mohawk won most of their fights with the French, and by about 1664 they had the Canadian colony practically at their mercy. One year later, King Louis XIV sent the famed Carnignan-Sallieres regiment to Canada. Under a new military governor, the Marquis de Tracy, the Carnignan attacked Mohawk country and destroyed several towns, while suffering plenty of casualties of its own. After this winter campaign, the Five Nations sued for peace, and a general agreement was reached at Quebec in 1667. If the

Converting the Mohawk

Though the Mohawk feared no one (admission of fear was virtually taboo), they recognized the French as their greatest foes. Sometimes this was because of the French skill in war, but just as often it was due to the influence and labors of Dominican friars and Jesuit priests.

Almost from the beginning of the Canadian colony, Jesuit (Society of Jesus) priests targeted the Mohawk for conversion to Roman Catholicism. Father Isaac Jogues and Father Lionel Brebeuf were the best known of a number of Frenchmen who came to minister to the Iroquois, and sometimes to live among them. As much as they detested the French colony—and the memory of Samuel de Champlain—the Mohawk had grudging admiration for the Jesuits, whom they labeled "Black Robes."

The Mohawk had a policy of never showing fear; the Jesuits had one of never giving up, no matter what the odds. Father Jogues, Father Brebeuf, and a handful of other priests died at the hands of the Mohawk after enduring severe forms of torture. These martyrdoms only increased the French desire to convert the Iroquois. By the last quarter of the seventeenth century, a significant number of Mohawk had converted to Catholicism, and they tended—like so many converts the world over—to be rigorous practitioners of their new faith. A Mohawk woman, Kateri Tekakwitha, underwent so many forms of humiliation and penance that followers launched a movement to make her the first Native American Catholic saint (she was beatified by Pope John Paul II in 1980).

Mohawk wished to chastise the French, they would need some powerful new allies.

COVENANT CHAIN

In the summer of 1677, the governors of New York and Virginia, along with a number of colonial commissioners, met at Albany with representatives of the Five Nations. No one spoke that much of the French, but it was collectively understood that this was an arrangement made for the security of the Five Nations and their English and Dutch neighbors. This conference, which launched the so-called Covenant Chain, was a major moment in Anglo-Iroquois diplomacy. A leading Iroquois sachem addressed the white leaders:

> We are very thankful to you, great sachem of Virginia, that you are pleased to be persuaded by Corlear, our governor, to forgive all former faults. We are very glad to hear you and to see your heart softened. Take these three beavers as a token.

Wampum belts were used by the Mohawk to mark important events. In fact, ceremonies were not considered official without the right wampum strings and treaties were not considered sealed unless a wampum belt was present. The belt shown above is either from the Iroquoian or Algonquian tribe, possibly from the seventeenth century.

The giving of beaver fur or wampum (shell) belts had become a traditional part of Mohawk diplomacy, and the governors of New York, Virginia, and Maryland were now accustomed to the practice. That session saw the swearing to a Covenant Chain between the Five Nations and their English and Dutch neighbors. No one mentioned the French, but it was plain that this alliance was primarily designed with them in mind.

There may have been an actual covenant chain made of silver or iron but the original deteriorated over time, and the Covenant Chain agreement became a symbolic one.

THE GREAT POWERS

For the next decade, the Five Nations were largely at peace. Then, in 1688, events in Europe conspired to change the fortunes of peoples in America.

In June 1688, the Catholic king and queen of England had a son—their first—which promised to continue their dynasty. Distressed over that possibility, leading English nobles and churchmen asked Princess Mary, who was married to the Dutch Prince William, to cross the English Channel and overthrow her father. William and Mary overthrew King James and Queen Mary in the autumn of 1688, and established their own Protestant dynasty.

The Mohawk rejoiced to hear the news, for in the persons of William and Mary they saw a union between the two European peoples whom they liked the best: English and Dutch. When they learned that England and Holland were at war with France, the Five Nations decided to strike the first blow. In August 1689, they descended on the village of La Chine, just outside Montreal, killing about 60 people and taking others captive. To the Mohawk, the destruction of French Canada seemed a real possibility.

IROQUOIS NAMES

By 1689, the Five Nations had a set of names for their European neighbors: Whoever was the mayor of nearby Albany was labeled

Quidor, an affectionate term based on the name of Colonel Peter Schuyler of Albany. Whoever was the governor in Manhattan was called *Corlear,* a transliteration of an early Dutchman's name. The French governor in Quebec was called *Onontio,* meaning "Great Mountain," and the colonists of Massachusetts were called *Kin-shon,* meaning "the fish" (they knew that the Massachusetts Puritans made their living from cod fishing).

In January 1690, about 80 sachems of the Five Nations met at Onondaga to discuss a set of peace proposals sent by the French Canadians. King Louis XIV had sent Count Frontenac over the ocean to govern Canada. The Iroquois already knew him, since he had been the governor a decade ago. He was a powerful military man with more than a trace of arrogance, often referring to American Indians as "my children." The 80 sachems listened intently during a council session that ran for many hours. At issue was whether they would remain neutral in the war between England and Holland on one side and France on the other, or if they would throw in with the English and Dutch.

The speeches were in the open, with everyone listening, but the debates among the sachems were quiet and subdued. Finally, the Onondaga sachem Sadenhaktie rose to give the answer:

> Brethren, we must stick to our Brother Quidor, and look on Onontio as our enemy for he is a cheat. . . . Corlear and Kinshon. Courage! Courage! In the spring to Quebec, take that place, and you'll have your feet on the necks of the French and all their friends in America.

The sachems had spoken.

The Coldest Time

Even though the Mohawk endured difficult, painful times in later years, they would always remember the late seventeenth and early eighteenth centuries as the time of greatest cold. They were correct: The decades between 1675 and 1725 were the deepest part of what we now call the Little Ice Age.

BLOOD IN THE SNOW

The Five Nations had voiced their contempt and anger for Onontio of Canada, but it was the French who struck the next big blow. On February 8, 1690, just weeks after the council fire at Onondaga, 114 French and their American Indian allies—80 Sault and 16 Algonquin Indians— set out from Montreal to attack settlements to the south. The group struck at the little town of Schenectady in the colony of New York. (*Schenectady,* a Mohawk word meaning "near the pines," had been Mohawk land and was settled by the Dutch in

In February 1690, the French and their Indian allies attacked the little town of Schenectady, New York. In this depiction, the snowmen standing guard at the open gate show the contempt the townspeople had for their far-off foes. The Mohawk were blamed for allowing the French and Indians to come so far into the province of New York.

1661.) They were retaliating for a series of Iroquois raids that the English had supported by providing guns and ammunition.

The French and the Canadian Indians virtually destroyed the place, killing about 60 people and taking many more captive to Canada. Albany received the grim news at nine o'clock that morning. The entire countryside was put on alert, but by the time the various militia groups had collected, the French and their allies were on their way back to Canada. The Mohawk knew that some of the blame would fall on them, for scouting the frontier and keeping the boundaries safe was part of their task.

CONDOLENCE

The rite of condolence was one of the most important of all rituals of the Five Nations. Two weeks after the destruction of

Schenectady, a number of Mohawk sachems came to Albany to express their sympathy with the Dutch.

Cadwallader Colden reported: "Brethren, the murder of our brethren at Schenectady by the French grieves us as much as if it had been done to ourselves. . . . We give this belt *to wipe away your tears* [emphasis in the original]." This was the first part of the ceremony, to cleanse the eyes of tears. Colden continued: "We don't think that what the French have done can be called a victory, it is only a further proof of their cruel deceit. . . . *We gather up our dead, to bury them,* by this second belt." No action could be undertaken until one had mourned one's losses: "*We give our brethren eye-water* to make them sharp sighted, giving a fourth belt." Then, the eyes must be cleansed and the ears cleared before one could make a good decision. Once it was made, however, the Mohawk would be firm allies in the quest for vengeance:

> Our chain is a strong chain, it is a silver chain, it can neither rust nor be broken. We, as to our parts, are resolute to continue the war. . . . We are of the race [clan] of the bear, and a bear you know never yields, while one drop of blood is left. *We must all be bears;* giving a sixth belt.

The war would continue.

ONONTIO'S WRATH

King William's War (named for the Dutchman who was England's new king) raged for eight years, with little real accomplishment on either side. Despite the Five Nations' admonition to Kinshon (Massachusetts) and Corlear (Manhattan) to eradicate the French colony, the war was a standoff. There were a few major battles, but the many skirmishes depleted the Five Nations' strength, with the Mohawk taking the worst losses.

In 1696, the 74-year-old Count Frontenac led a French invasion of Five Nations territory (the aged count had to be carried in a litter). The French came into the land of the Onondaga, uprooting crops and burning corn where it stood. Rather few Onondaga or Frenchmen died in this campaign, but it showed an increased power on the part of the French, and the Mohawk and their kinsmen took notice. By 1698, when peace was declared, the Five Nations were in desperate need of recuperation.

PEACE OF MONTREAL

In the next three years, the Mohawk reconsidered their traditional alliance with the English. Though they would never ally with the French, the Mohawk and the other Five Nations considered making peace with Canada and standing neutral in any future conflict. Seizing upon this, the new French governor (Count Frontenac had died in 1698) invited sachems from the Five Nations and the Great Lakes region to Montreal for a great conference to bury the hatchet.

The French-language book *Planter l'Arbre de Paix* ("Planting the Tree of Peace") shows the pictorial signatures of 36 American Indian chiefs. The Kahnawake Mohawk were represented by l'Aigle, and those of the Lake of the Mountain by a chief named Tsahouanhos. The Mohawk of the river valley were represented by a chief named Agniers, but he declined to affix his mark to the final treaty. Perhaps this was a final gesture of defiance, but there is little doubt that the Mohawk, whether in Canada or the American colonies, wanted peace.

The Peace of Montreal, signed in the summer of 1701, declared the Five Nations' neutrality for whatever lay ahead.

QUEEN ANNE'S WAR

King William died in 1702. His wife, Queen Mary, had died several years earlier. The couple had no children, so the British throne passed to Mary's sister, Anne, who thus became queen.

Even before William's death, Britain and France had been once again heading towards conflict. The new war, declared in 1702, was dubbed Queen Anne's War by the American colonists. (Europeans called it the War of the Spanish Succession.) When they learned of this new conflict, the Mohawk and other Five Nations were less than pleased. No sooner had they worked out a deal with the French, than the British once more started a conflict. Were it not for the presence of the Kahnawake Mohawk to the north, the

Old Deerfield Captives

About 100 miles (160 kilometers) east of the Mohawk River Valley, historic Deerfield is one of the best preserved of any eighteenth-century site. Located in a river valley of its own, Deerfield was a small but prosperous Puritan community when the French and their American Indian allies (Abenaki as well as Kahnawake Mohawk) attacked on February 29, 1704.

The French came because they were fighting the English, and the Abenaki came because they were allies of the French; the Kahnawake Mohawk came because of a church bell. The year before, a French ship carrying a bell intended for the Kahnawake Catholic Church had been captured, and the church bell had been sold at an auction in Massachusetts. Reverend John Williams purchased the bell and brought it to Deerfield.

The French, Abenaki, and Kahnawake swarmed over Deerfield that morning, killing many and taking about 110 people captive. Among them were Reverend Williams, his wife, and several of their children. Many books have been written and numerous paintings done of the painful trip to Canada, depicting piles of snow resembling mountains. Mrs. Williams, weak from recent childbirth, was killed by the American Indians early into the march. Her husband and children all reached Canada, where some were held captive by the French and others by the American Indians.

After two years of captivity, Reverend Williams and most of his family were ransomed. They went by ship to Boston, where he delivered a famous sermon that became the basis

Mohawk Valley Indians might have remained neutral in the war. Their hand was forced by their countrymen north of the border.

Because of the raid on Deerfield and subsequent border fights, the Mohawk became involved in Queen Anne's War, albeit to a

for his best-selling book *The Redeemed Captive Returned to Zion*. Williams and his family returned to Deerfield, which had been rebuilt, and they reentered their earlier life as pillars of the community, and as leaders of the Connecticut River Valley Puritans.

One of the Williamses had been left behind, however. Eunice Williams had been only four years old when Deerfield was attacked, and the Kahnawake Mohawk took a great liking to her. Mohawk River Valley Indians and their Canadian cousins alike took as many captives as possible, and adopted the most promising ones as a way to replenish their numbers. When the time for ransoming came, they would not let Eunice go. She, too, had become very fond of her captors. Years later, when she was asked why she would not return to Deerfield, she suggested that the reason was that her father had remarried too quickly, that he had not significantly honored the memory of her mother. Given that she was now a Mohawk (they named her "she who brings in the corn"), Eunice may have felt the need for an extended condolence ceremony.

John Williams died, and leadership of the family passed to his son Stephen, also a Puritan pastor. In midlife, Stephen kept in contact with his younger sister, and on at least two occasions, she and her Mohawk husband came all the way south to visit with him. She expressed much affection for her white family, but said she needed to sleep outdoors: The Puritan houses were too confining for her spirit.

A woman of two worlds, Eunice Williams remains one of the most intriguing of colonial characters. She saw the good, the bad, and the ugly of Puritan and Mohawk life, and she lived to the ripe age of 89.

lesser extent than before. It took all the anxious labors of Colonel Peter Schuyler of Albany (they had converted his first name to *Quidor*) to persuade the Mohawk to take a greater interest in the war. In 1709, after a planned British invasion of Canada failed to get off the ground, Colonel Schuyler persuaded four leading Northeast sachems (three Mohawk and one Mohican) to accompany him to London to work their magic on Queen Anne. Schuyler's urging led to the biggest stage for the Mohawk people yet seen, and to a lasting impression made upon the people of London, who called them the "Four Mohawk Kings." Thanks to the research of Richmond P. Bond and to the engravings of John Verelst, we have a good idea of what the American Indian leaders looked like.

FOUR KINGS, ONE QUEEN

The "Emperor of the Six Nations" appears before us in the engraving by John Verelst (whose Native American name was *Tejonihokarawa,* or "open the door"). A tall man with a serious look, the engraving's subject wears European-style clothing, including a handsome pair of leggings, and shoes that look as if they were made in Holland. Only a blanket draped around his shoulder betrays his heritage. The "Emperor" (though he would not have claimed or recognized that title) stands in a woodland scene, with a wolf behind his right leg. The wolf shows his clan status. The Emperor holds a large belt of wampum with 12 distinct crosses stitched upon it. The symbolic importance of the number 12 is not known. Only when the viewer looks down to the far right of the scene does he or she see a tomahawk that lies there, discarded, a sign that the Emperor has come in peace.

The "King of the Generethgarich" is not as tall or commanding as the Emperor. He, too, stands in a woodland scene, and he holds a bow in his left hand, but his gesture and facial expression are anything but threatening. Unlike the black shoes of the Emperor, the King wears silk moccasins, a subtle reminder that even the most prized of Native American artifacts could be transformed by whites. A wolf lurks behind his left leg.

In April 1710, four Indian chiefs representing the Five Nations traveled to Great Britain to meet with Queen Anne. They hoped to secure support against the French and their Native American allies. They were treated like royalty everywhere they went, and some 30 portraits were painted. Right is a depiction of King of the River Nations; left is Emperor of the Six Nations.

The "King of the Maquas" is the tallest of the four: He fills his portrait scene vertically. His traditional clothing (mixed with silk moccasins) is open at the chest, allowing the viewer to see his handsome, vertically striped tattoos. In his right hand, the King holds the barrel of a long musket, which might be a prototype of the famous Kentucky rifle. Though a tomahawk lies on the ground, his overall gesture is commanding, and the large black bear by his left leg is menacing.

The "King of the River Nation" is the least threatening of the four. Though he carries a war club in his right hand and has a European-style sword strapped to his belt, this King seems the least mature and dangerous of the group. Perhaps that is the artist's way of telling us that he belongs to the River (Mahican) Nation, rather than the feared Mohawk. A tortoise crawls by his right foot.

The Four "Kings" met Queen Anne on April 20, 1710.

THE SPEECH

The Kings did not speak English, but they had composed a speech, which was read aloud to Queen Anne. (The speech is preserved in Richmond P. Bond's *Queen Anne's American Kings*.) What she thought of these men from across the ocean is difficult to say, but the idea of the "Noble Savage" (a person unexposed to the weaknesses and vanities of Western civilization) was growing in European consciousness at the time.

> Great Queen!
> We have undertaken a long and tedious voyage, which none of our predecessors could ever be prevailed upon to undertake. The motive that induced us was, that we might see our Great Queen, and relate to her those things we thought absolutely necessary for the good of her and us her allies, on the other side [of] the great water.

Anne had been queen for seven years, and she was no doubt experienced with the flattery of courtiers and diplomats, but she may not have realized that for these American Indians, the sight of a woman in power was not unusual. The Five Nations had long revered clan mothers as the heads of their government.

> We doubt not but our Great Queen has been acquainted with our long and tedious war, in conjunction with her children [meaning subjects] against her enemies the French; and that we have been as a strong wall for their security, even to the loss of our best men.

This was more debatable. Queen Anne's War had raged for eight years, but the Mohawk and other Five Nations had been less than a "strong wall." Generally, they had kept as neutral as they could.

> We need not urge to our Great Queen, more than the necessity we really labor under obliges us, that in case our Great Queen should not be mindful of us, we must, with our families, forsake

our country and seek other habitations, or stand neuter; either of which will be much against our inclinations.

Two generations earlier, this threat would have been laughable, for everyone knew how attached the Mohawk were to their beloved river valley. But, given that some Mohawk had already migrated north to Kahnawake and the Lake of the Mountain, it seemed quite possible that these leaders, too, might forsake the British cause. What the sachems wanted was a firm commitment from the queen that she would send a British fleet and army to join them in the conquest of Canada. After some time delivering more flattering words about the Christian religion and their desire to have Anglican (Church of England) missionaries sent, the Mohawk leaders withdrew. They had made a strong impression.

NOBLE SAVAGE

For the six weeks they were in town, the American Indians were the sensation of London. The British press followed them everywhere, noted their clan dignity, and asked all sorts of questions that could not be answered because of the language difference. By the time the sachems departed for Boston and then home, they continued to be a topic of conversation. For the next generation, Londoners thought of *Mohawk* and *Indian* as almost synonymous, and many literary references were made to the "noble savages" who had crossed the Atlantic to see the queen.

All the diplomacy came to nothing, however. Queen Anne did send a fleet and army, but several British transport ships went aground in the mouth of the St. Lawrence River. After seeing about 700 of his men drowned, the British admiral turned and headed for home. The conquest of Canada—so important in the Mohawk mind—would not happen during this phase of the French and American Indian wars.

Our Wise Forefathers

The degree to which the Iroquois Confederacy was used as a model by the U.S. Founding Fathers in 1787 remains the subject of debate. Some scholars are convinced that Benjamin Franklin, for one, used the Iroquois as his model, while others believe that the Six Nations were only a minor inspiration.

FIVE TO SIX

In 1722, after about 10 years of migration, the Tuscarora—an Iroquoian-speaking people from North Carolina—became the sixth member of the Iroquois Nation. The Mohawk were already the "people of the flint," and the Oneida were called the "people of the great stone." The Tuscarora received the name "shirt-wearers," which apparently indicates their previous close relationship with the white peoples of North and South Carolina.

The Tuscarora were "adopted" by the Seneca and given some lands in upstate New York, but they never became a senior member of the Council of Six Nations. Their appearance was both a sign of weakness of the Southern Woodland tribes, and a signal that the Iroquois were seen as one of the few hopes for resisting the power of the white Europeans. Even the Six Nations were losing lands, however.

GERMANS

In the same year that Queen Anne welcomed the four sachems to London, a large group of German refugees called the Palatines went to Manhattan as the first step in finding new lands to settle. Queen Anne had taken these refugees from the war named in her honor, and directed them to the province of New York. This settled them in the lower Mohawk River Valley, and was one of the first, and by no means last, of a series of white migrations that pushed the Six Nations hard. Just as the Mohawk had suffered the greatest American Indian casualties during the last two wars, so too did they lose the greatest number of acres to the new immigrants. At an earlier time, the Mohawk might have turned on the whites, uprooting their settlements, but by 1720 it was clear that the English, Dutch, Swedes, and Germans of New York were far too many to be defeated. The Six Nations had to live with their new neighbors.

CULTURAL CHANGES

The Mohawk of 1720 or 1730 were not the same as their grandmothers and grandfathers; three generations of cultural contact had wrought many changes. By the opening of the eighteenth century, a fair number of Mohawk lived in European-style cabins and homes, rather than the traditional longhouses, and some wore a good deal of European-style clothing. (Some of this was witnessed by the dress of the "Four Mohawk Kings" in London.) Because of the prevalence of liquor in the white trading posts, some Mohawk became helpless alcoholics.

The changes the Mohawk experienced are described by Lois M. Huey and Bonnie Pulis in their biography of Molly Brant:

> The Mohawk adapted to change by accepting those practices that seemed to make their lives better. They maintained traditions and beliefs, and grafted to them new ideas that proved useful. The longhouse did not disappear, as families moved to smaller houses, but became the center for ceremonial life. Guns largely replaced the bow and arrow. Copper kettles proved more durable than clay pots. . . . These adaptations were occurring throughout Iroquoia, but the Mohawk, located closest to white settlements, had embraced them to a greater extent by the 1750s than others in the Confederacy.

It was around this time that the Mohawk met a white man who would become their greatest champion.

WILLIAM JOHNSON

He was born in County Meath, Ireland, in 1714 to a Roman Catholic family of stature, which made his opportunities for advancement difficult in the British Empire. Johnson's uncle, Sir Peter Warren, was raised as a Protestant, so Warren was able to rise in the British Royal Navy. Not particularly religious, Johnson converted to Protestantism and came to America with the task of managing his uncle's estates in the lower Mohawk Valley. When he first arrived in 1738, Johnson stayed on the southern side of the Mohawk River, organizing his uncle's land patents and encouraging German (Palatine) settlers to come. He married one of them, Catharine Weisenberger.

About four years later, Johnson moved north of the Mohawk River to establish Fort Johnson, in present-day Johnstown, New York. Intent on becoming his own man, Johnson spent only part of his time with his uncle's estates, and concentrated upon becoming

Sir William Johnson
Major General of the English Forces in America

Publish'd According to Act of Parliam.ᵗ 2 Feb.ʳ 1756. And sold by W.ᵐ Herbert under y Piazzas on London Bridge

Sir William Johnson had a long history with the Mohawk. At age 23, Johnson moved to the undeveloped land near the Mohawk River and lived among the tribe. He learned the Mohawk language and customs and served as their New York agent. The Mohawk even adopted him as an honorary sachem.

the biggest merchant of up-colony New York. His most recent biographer, Fintan O'Toole, believes that coming of age in an Ireland split between Catholic and Protestant was a help to Johnson: He adjusted well to life on the New York frontier and was able to tread the narrow ground between American Indians and whites. Within about 10 years of his arrival, Johnson had become an honorary Mohawk chief, and he seemed as comfortable in traditional dress as in Irish or English clothing.

Recent historians have pointed out that Johnson feathered his own nest quite nicely, using his unique position to increase and develop a vast set of landholdings in New York. The Mohawk saw him as their best white friend, however, and labeled him *Warahinginey,* meaning "he who does much business."

Johnson's Love Life

Because of his position on the frontier between Europeans and American Indians, and thanks to a number of books (both fictional and historical), Johnson has developed the reputation of a ladies' man. Some authors have even suggested that he had a harem, with a different Mohawk woman for every night of the year. This is unlikely because, as historian Francis Jennings puts it, "there were not that many in existence."

Johnson lived a few miles north of the river in a Georgian mansion that he called Johnson Hall. It was the most impressive in the countryside. Everyone who left a record of his or her visit there wrote that Johnson was constantly entertaining. As he put it in a letter to a friend, "my house is always full of Indians." The tobacco smoke rose, the brandy circulated, and the conversations went on, hour after hour until about three in the morning, when everyone went to sleep. It

CAUGHT IN THE MIDDLE

For much of their history, the Six Nations were caught between the British and Dutch to the east and the French to the north. In the early eighteenth century, it became apparent that there was another player: the governors of Pennsylvania, whose lands crept up from the south onto those of the Mohawk.

William Penn had founded Pennsylvania in 1682 on principles of fair play and justice, but his sons and grandsons did not act that way. Through a set of treaties, usually negotiated in Philadelphia, the Penn family increased its landholdings and the size of the colony. Witnessing the growing strength of Pennsylvania, the Six Nations undertook a series of negotiations with the governors of New York, Pennsylvania, and Virginia. This led to an

is understandable how myths of female companions would develop around this lifestyle, but Johnson seemed much too busy acting as host and interpreter, and also as land-bargainer, to spend much time with different Mohawk women.

Johnson's first wife was Catherine Weisenberger, a German Palatine about whom little is known. Together they had four children, who were named as Johnson's principal heirs. Not long after her death, Johnson took up with Molly Brant, a Mohawk woman who had been raised in nearby Canajoharie. They never officially married. She was his principal housekeeper (a very big task at Johnson Hall) and was recognized as the second most important person in white-Indian relations in the region. They had eight children, all of whom were generously provided for in Johnson's will.

No one would want to remove all the mystery from Johnson's days as the fire keeper on the frontier. He may well have had other liaisons, about which little is known, and he may have had more than the 12 children from his two relationships. The idea that he was some sort of American Casanova, however, is greatly exaggerated.

unprecedented amount of printed material, detailing the speeches and actions of the leading Six Nations sachems. Much of the source material went to Philadelphia, where an ambitious young printer by the name of Benjamin Franklin printed it for the public. Franklin was only in his thirties when he became aware of the speech-making qualities of the Six Nations chiefs, and the knowledge he gained would play a part in his role as a Founding Father of the United States. Historian after historian and anthropologist after anthropologist have pointed out the important speech made at Lancaster, Pennsylvania, in 1744 by the Seneca chief Canassatego.

Toward the end of the conference, which lasted two weeks, the Onondaga sachem Canassatego rose to remind everyone of the importance of the Covenant Chain, which had been forged between the Six Nations and the Anglo colonists. He had a few words of advice for the people of the 13 fires (as the colonists were called):

> We heartily recommend union and a good agreement between you our brethren. Never disagree, but preserve a strict friendship for one another, and thereby you, as well as we, will become the stronger.
>
> *Our wise forefathers* [emphasis added] established union and amity between the Five Nations; this has made us formidable; this has given us great weight and authority with our neighboring nations.
>
> We are a powerful confederacy; and, by observing the same methods [that] *our wise forefathers* [emphasis added] have taken, you will acquire fresh strength and power; therefore, whatever befalls you, never fall out with another.

Benjamin Franklin printed Canassatego's words, which later became part of *Indian Treaties,* published in Philadelphia. Though no one called attention to it at the time, Canassatego's use of the words "wise forefathers" closely resembled the later term "founding fathers," used to describe the individuals who founded the United States. Perhaps the Franklin connection made the words

In this illustration by Native American artist John Fadden, Canassatego delivers a speech at the Lancaster Treaty Council in 1744. During this meeting, Canassatego urged the colonies, which had no central authority, to form a union similar to the Iroquois. Ben Franklin published transcripts of the treaty, including Canassatego's speech, in small booklets.

known to many people; whatever the cause, thousands of people have read the Onondaga chieftain's words, and have pondered what meaning they may have had for the U.S. Constitution.

KING GEORGE'S WAR

War between England and France broke out in 1744, and the American colonists were quick to play a part. Massachusetts militiamen captured French Fort Louisbourg on Cape Breton Island, and French-Canadian militia and their Abenaki allies attacked several New England frontier towns. The Six Nations were not eager to participate in this conflict. An unwritten rule was established, whereby the French and their American Indian allies purposely avoided attacking New York, thereby keeping the Mohawk in a state of virtual neutrality.

When the war ended in 1748, the peace treaty of Aix-la-Chapelle returned all lands and properties to the country that had possessed them before the conflict began. The return of Louisbourg to France enraged many New England colonists. Some historians see that anger as the beginning—however small—of an eventual move toward American independence. Other historians point to 1754 as pivotal in the development of a colonial American identity.

FRANKLIN AND UNION

Historians have long pointed to Benjamin Franklin (in his forties at the time of King George's War) as the architect of the Albany Plan of Union. Historian Timothy J. Shannon, however, gives the credit to the Mohawk in his landmark *At the Crossroads of Empire.* One year earlier, in 1753, Mohawk Chief Hendrik—who was closely aligned with William Johnson—had gone to Albany to demand to see the governor of New York. In a short confer-ence, which lacked the usual formalities of gift-giving, Hendrik claimed that he and the Mohawk were disgusted with the greed of the Albany merchants, English and Dutch alike. If *Corlear* (the name for the New York governor) could not control his people and prevent them from taking over Mohawk lands, then the Covenant Chain, which dated back to 1677, would be broken. This was the most drastic diplomatic action a Mohawk had taken in decades.

British officials in London quickly sent out messages to the northern colonies, insisting that the traditional alliance with the Six Nations be maintained. Given that the Mohawk were the clos-est to Albany and had the longest tradition of relationships with the whites, it was imperative to have them on the Anglo-American side. As Timothy J. Shannon expressed it:

> The Albany conference, held in the summer of 1754, embellished and shined the Covenant Chain between the Anglo settlers and the Six Nations. Hendrik attended, and received more presents

from William Johnson and other colonial officials than in the past. Even so, there was a sense of urgency, for if the Mohawk could not be trusted fully, the entire Anglo-American frontier was in danger.

Shannon continues:

> In the mid-eighteenth century, the Mohawk Valley was an axis of empire, a borderland between the continent's British, French, and Native American inhabitants. . . . Despite their reputation as warriors, the Mohawks' power had always rested in their role as diplomatic gatekeepers between Albany and the western Indians.

If the Mohawk continued to be deprived of this role—thanks to the relentless westward movement of the white settlers—they would be much less important to the British or the French. Knowing this made Hendrik uneasy, and led the Mohawk to demand more gifts from the British, more assurances that the Covenant Chain would remain unbroken.

The Longhouse Divides

Until about the year 1755, the twin concepts of the Great Peace and the Longhouse (symbolic rather than literal), under which Iroquois would not fight Iroquois, held very well. Even after 1755, the concept struggled on for another generation, but the opening of the American Revolutionary War spelled doom for the confederacy.

BRADDOCK AND JOHNSON

In the spring of 1755, Great Britain and France were on the edge of war, though it would not be formally declared until 1756. Both nations sent reinforcements to their American colonies, with orders to secure forts and deprive the enemy of supplies and communications.

British general Edward Braddock landed in Maryland in the spring, and by early summer he was headed west to seize French Fort Duquesne, in modern-day Pittsburgh, Pennsylvania. His

SOI·EN·GA·RAH·TA,

OR

KING HENDRICK.

The Iroquois fought on the English side during the wars with the French. Still, the English settlers encroached on Mohawk land, ignoring Iroquois' rights. Chief Hendrick and 16 Mohawk men traveled to meet with New York's Governor Clinton and threatened to break the Covenant Chain.

army was mostly British, with many red-coated veterans of European campaigns. The young George Washington was one of his scouts and American advisers. As they neared their destination, the British felt confident of victory.

The French and their American Indian allies—a mixture of Abenaki, Ohio, and Great Lakes tribes—ambushed General Braddock and his men on July 8, 1755, just a few miles from Fort Duquesne. Braddock fought bravely but died; his straight-on approach to military matters was a catastrophe for both his men and the Anglo-American cause. George Washington escaped with a coat full of bullet holes, but lived to fight another day. The news spread up and down the frontier that the French and their allies were on the loose.

The Two Hendriks

For generations, Americans have mistakenly believed that the Chief Hendrik who fought and died at the Battle of Lake George was the same who had gone to London in 1710. Thanks to the detailed genealogical research of Barbara J. Sivertsen, we now know this to be false.

John Verelst's 1710 engravings provided the first important clues. The "Emperor of the Six Nations," as Hendrik is titled, is clearly a man of maturity, perhaps between 40 and 50 years old. If he was that old in 1711, Hendrik would have been in his eighties or nineties when asked to lead the Mohawk into battle in 1755. Despite the clear incongruity, scholars continued to accept the idea that he had done so.

In 1996, Barbara Sivertsen's research was published. *Turtles, Wolves, and Bears: A Mohawk Family History* was a path-breaking work because it showed the lineages of many

In the same season that Braddock set out, William Johnson held a huge council fire at Albany, a break with the Onondaga council fire tradition. Johnson gave impassioned speeches in English and Mohawk, calling on all the Six Nations to demonstrate their loyalty to King George II, and to hold fast to the Covenant Chain. Johnson's oratory persuaded all the Six Nations to declare allegiance to the British, but only the Mohawk sent a sizeable contingent of warriors, led by Chief Hendrik.

By early September, the colonists and Mohawk were at the foot of Lake George, poised for a strike northward along Lake George and Lake Champlain. The French beat them to the punch, however, and on the morning of September 8, William Johnson and Hendrik learned that the French and their American Indian

important Mohawk families, including those of the two Hendriks. In the spring of 1690, the Dutch Reformed minister at Albany baptized a handful of Mohawk, his first converts. Among them was "Tejonihokarawa, i.e. Open the door, about 30 years old, now called Henderick."

This confirms that the engraving of 1710 was correct in its portrayal of a man who had indeed weathered about 50 winters. But Sivertsen's research takes us further, and we learn that this Hendrik died sometime after 1735. His place in the Mohawk hierarchy was taken by another Hendrik, a Canajoharie Mohawk who went to England in 1740 and met with King George II. This second Hendrik was the man who mustered the Mohawk in 1755 and fought with William Johnson at the Battle of Lake George.

Some might claim that this slow discovery is an example of historians and genealogists taking great pains over small matters, but to be able to tell the difference between the Hendrik of 1710 and the other of 1755 is an enormous step forward in our understanding of the Mohawk people.

allies—including a group of Caughnawaga Mohawk—were in the vicinity. The war council voted to send a detachment of 1,500 men into the woods to scout the enemy's position. Chief Hendrik registered his opposition, saying that if they were to fight, they were too few, and that if they were to die, they were too many. Despite his argument, he was overruled, and in the end accepted leadership of the column.

Just a mile out from the safe location, the French and their allies attacked the column in an eerie replica of what had happened to Braddock's army two months earlier. Chief Hendrik—one of the few men who was on horseback—was killed in the early moments of the fighting, which sometimes had northern Mohawk fighting southern ones. In his doctoral dissertation in anthropology, David S. Blanchard describes the meeting between the different groups of natives:

> In this confusion, a Mohawk warrior happened to encounter his friend, a Caughnawaga [Kahnawake], they saluted one another, and shook hands. In the meantime another came up—who was making a blow at the Mohawk—the latter parried it and killed him, a second instantly rushed on, making a similar attempt, he killed him also; his friend stood by a passive spectator of the slaughter of his comrades; so strong was the bond of friendship that even when meeting in hostile array, it obliged them to spare one another. The Caughnawaga [Kahnawake] then exclaimed: 'Oh my friend, we have met in disagreeable circumstances—let us part.'

So they did, while others—Native and European alike—slaughtered one another in what was called the "Bloody Scout."

The French and American Indians won the morning encounter, but the British colonials and their allies won the afternoon bout, which saw the former attack the latter's campsite. Though there were marked displays of affection—such as that registered by Blanchard—the day witnessed the first wholesale combat between Six Nations warriors in hundreds of years. This break did not destroy the Iroquois longhouse, but it impaired it.

Though he had won an important victory, Johnson was unable to follow it up. He kept his force at Lake George for another month, then sent the men and warriors home for the winter. Even though he had not come within a hundred miles of Canada, Johnson won the only significant victory achieved by British arms that year, and a grateful King George II made him a baronet. *Sir* William Johnson was now, truly, a man of two worlds.

FIGHT TO THE FINISH

The French and Indian War officially began with the exchange of declarations in May 1756. By then, the French seemed to have the upper hand in the conflict.

Outnumbered by about 20 to 1, the French and their American Indian allies nonetheless had the advantage of interior lines of communication, and they won important victories at Fort Oswego in 1756 and at Fort William Henry in 1757. The latter battle, or siege, is one of the best known of all frontier fights, both because of the colorful imagery around the setting and because of the tragic massacre of 200 people after they had surrendered. The siege was a victory for the French and their American Indian allies, but it came at a high price, because the American colonists became convinced that nothing less than total victory in the war was acceptable.

The tide of the war changed in 1758. The British sent new generals and larger armies to America, and in 1758 they captured both Louisbourg, on the coast of Cape Breton Island, and Fort Duquesne. A year later, they captured Quebec, and in 1760, Montreal fell to their arms as well. The Mohawk benefited little during this turnaround in British-American fortunes. Some served under Sir William Johnson in the capture of Fort Niagara, and some Caughnawaga Mohawk found employment as boatmen for General Jeffrey Amherst's campaign against Montreal. On the whole, however, the Six Nations found little

The July 8, 1755, ambush of General Braddock and his men was one of the biggest victories for the French and their Indian allies. In this illustration, General Braddock falls from his horse, a musket ball lodged in his chest. The painting shows the superior war skills of the French and Indians, who hid behind natural obstacles in order to defeat the column of red-coated British soldiers.

of comfort. Even the complete British victory, sealed with the Peace of Paris, did little to improve the Mohawk's situation, for now there was only one European power—Great Britain—and no one else with whom the Mohawk could engage in power play.

PROCLAMATION OF 1763

In the same year that the Peace of Paris confirmed the British conquest of Canada, King George III drew a line on a map (with, as one historian described it, "the scratch of a pen"), forbidding his white American colonists to move beyond the ridge of the Appalachian Mountains. King George had good reason to believe that the American Indians would be more manageable if his American colonists ceased pressing land claims to the west. The Proclamation was too late to save the Mohawk, however, for they were mostly settled in the valley that bisected the Appalachian Mountains. There was no safety for their lands.

BROTHER JOHNSON

The Mohawk turned to the only white person they trusted: Sir William Johnson. At the peak of his powers, Johnson was now practically a land baron, as well as an American Indian agent and keeper of the council fire at Johnson Hall. He was willing to do much to help his Mohawk friends, but there was always a price—however subtle—for his assistance. Johnson continued to expand his land holdings, while arranging and then leading the negotiations of the Fort Stanwix Treaty of 1768. Johnson emerged more powerful than ever, but his Mohawk friends were at the end of their rope. Two generations ago, they might have broken the white settlers with fire and sword. One generation earlier, they might have prevailed in a council negotiation. But now, in 1768, they were powerless against the onslaught of fur trappers, merchants, and an endless stream of white settlers. All the Mohawk could do was watch as yet another dramatic clash began to unfold: the growing separation between Britain and the 13 colonies.

LEAD-UP TO REVOLUTION

In 1768, the year of the Fort Stanwix Treaty, England and its colonies were still entwined in a political and cultural mesh that had endured for a century and a half. As King George and Parliament attempted to crack down on the colonies by laying new taxes and customs duties, the relationship began to unravel. First came the Stamp Act of 1765, then the Townshend revenue acts of 1767, then the Boston Massacre of 1770. None of these events had any impact on the Mohawk, 200 miles (320 km) away, but the Boston Tea Party of 1773 had definite reverberations. For reasons unknown to

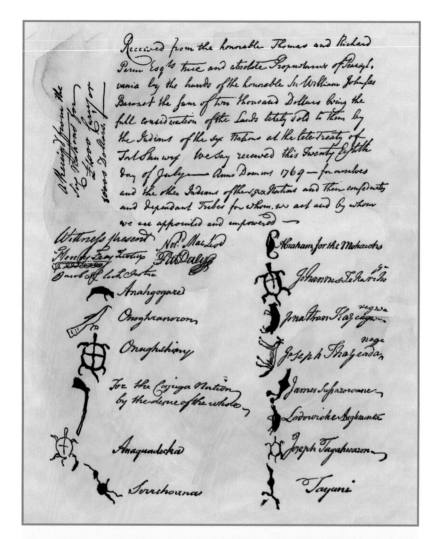

In 1769, the British signed a treaty with the Six Nations for large portions of land. This document features the original handwriting of the important chiefs. Note the signature of Joseph Thayendega on the right side.

most, the men involved in the Boston Tea Party dressed as American Indians (Mohawk no less) and most newspapers reported that they were the fierce and rebellious men of the frontier, rather than the merchants and artisans that they were. Many historians have pondered the matter, but none came up with a convincing answer until 2008, when Roger D. Abrahams discussed his research in the online magazine *Common Place:*

> These terms were far from new. They came into use at the spectacular and unexpected arrival of our Mohawk "ambassadors" to the court of Queen Anne . . . They were encountered by many Londoners, not only those who officially received them at court. . . . After this visit, the word Mohawk took on a life of its own. Rumors began to spread of a night-marauding group of the Hellfire sort made up of young swells called "Mohocks and Hawkubites."

Whether the "Mohawk" of eighteenth century London did any real damage is beside the point. By 1773, when the Bostonians threw the tea into the harbor, *Mohawk* had become synonymous with a frightening person of the night doing nefarious deeds.

The Boston Tea Party was decisive, driving a breach between Britain and the colonies. By the spring of 1774, Boston Harbor was blockaded by the British, and war between America and its parent nation seemed possible, perhaps likely.

A LEADER PASSES

In the early summer of 1774, a large delegation of Six Nations sachems came to Johnson Hall, which had almost replaced Onondaga as the site of major council fires. Sir William Johnson heard many complaints from the American Indians, most of them centered around local white settlers plundering the land. As cited in Vol. 2 of *Documentary History of New York*, the chief of the Canajoharie Mohawk made a special appeal:

> Brother
> It is with pain I am under the necessity of complaining again against that old rogue, the old disturber of our village, George Klock. You are long acquainted with his artifices, and evil conduct, and you have often assured us you had applied the redress; but whatever is the reason, we never yet obtained any satisfaction

Johnson had heard the complaints before, and sometimes he sounded both defensive and weary in reply. The painful truth was that he had no remedy. The white settlers—English, German, Dutch, and others—had the upper hand in their relations with the Mohawk, whose lands were doomed to decrease.

In the early afternoon, Johnson begged to rest for a while, and was soothing his headache with some fresh tea, when he died suddenly. He was only 60. The Mohawk were shocked. Brother Johnson, Chief Much Business, had been the only white person they really trusted. He had an heir, Sir John Johnson, but the American Indians were beside themselves with grief, for Johnson had been their ally and best friend in an increasingly perilous world.

LEXINGTON AND CONCORD

On April 19, 1775, the Revolution commenced with the battles of Lexington and Concord. News reached the Mohawk Valley a week later, and the Mohawk were placed in a dilemma: Should they support King George and Britain, or the 13 colonies that they called the 13 fires?

Had Johnson lived, virtually all the Mohawk and also the great majority of the other Iroquois would have supported the king. Johnson was a devoted royalist. His death removed the strongest pro-British force on the frontier.

Had the Oneida not been won over to the American side by Reverend Samuel Kirkland—a Presbyterian missionary from Connecticut—the Six Nations might have remained a united force through the war. Kirkland was a devoted patriot, and his sermons helped to win over at least half the Oneida for the revolutionary cause.

Mohawk had first fought Mohawk at the Battle of Lake George in 1755. Now, 20 years later, they would do so again. This time, the whole Six Nations would be split by quarrels in the white people's world.

Thirteen
Versus One

The 13 fires and King George, across the ocean, went to war in the spring of 1775. Practically all of the Six Nations people wanted to stay out of what they saw as a family quarrel between the king and his colonies. Not even the most aggressive Mohawk warriors wished to get involved in what was clearly a struggle for political supremacy among the whites. The defeat of the French in the French and Indian War had given a clear lesson to the Iroquois: It was better to play off two great powers than to encounter one only.

Because of their connection to the Johnson family, a majority of the Mohawk favored the British cause. Thanks to their connection with a Connecticut missionary, many of the Oneida came to support the revolutionary Americans. This division made life in the Iroquois Longhouse shaky indeed.

REVEREND KIRKLAND

Samuel Kirkland was a Presbyterian missionary who came west to minister to the Oneida in the 1760s. Right from the beginning, he was seen as a challenge to Johnson's influence. The two men cordially despised one another.

At the age of 15, Joseph Brant took part in several battles of the French and Indian War, receiving a medal from the British for his services. He was persuaded to fight for the British during the American Revolution.

When the Revolutionary War began, Reverend Kirkland took a group of Oneida sachems on a journey to Philadelphia to meet the delegates of the Second Continental Congress. This was the first of a series of steps by which he won the Oneida over to the American cause. A man of great sincerity and depth, Kirkland was able to persuade the Oneida that siding with the revolutionaries was in their best interest.

Completely on the other side of the equation was Joseph Brant, also known as Thayendenaga. The younger brother of Molly Brant, he had grown up at Johnson Hall, and was educated in a colonial school in Connecticut. When the war began, Brant was inclined to support the British side. He became fully convinced of this when the American revolutionaries invaded British Canada.

THE FOURTEENTH COLONY

In the autumn of 1775, two American armies attacked British Canada, which had been known as French Canada until just 15 years earlier. The first army, led by Benedict Arnold (who later became the most notorious traitor in U.S. history), went by way of Maine to attack Quebec City. The second, led by General Richard Montgomery, crossed the border to attack Montreal.

Joseph Brant, Daniel Claus, and a handful of other Johnson Hall loyalists were in Montreal at the time of the American attack. They got out of the town and to Quebec before Montreal surrendered, and then took ship for England. The Americans captured Montreal and came within a hairsbreadth of taking Quebec City, but their narrow failure allowed the British to not only hold on to the city, but also paved the way for them to retake all of Canada in the spring.

Joseph Brant was lionized during this, his first stay in London. The artist George Romney painted his portrait and he met King George III, whom he found a most admirable person. (Brant later said he could not imagine why anyone would rebel against such a virtuous leader.) The London journalists clung to Brant as fiercely as their predecessors had done with the Four Mohawk Kings of 1710.

Indeed, to some, Brant seemed like a second coming of the "noble savage." His winter stay in London convinced Brant of the power and virtue of the British cause, and when he returned to America it was as a confirmed loyalist, one ready to shed blood on behalf of the king and Parliament.

MANHATTAN

In the late summer of 1776, Brant was in the British-Hessian army that captured New York City from the Americans. This, one of the greatest British victories of the war, made England's eventual triumph seem certain, and Brant went to upstate New York to recruit Mohawk and other Six Nations warriors for the British cause. By the time he arrived, the Johnsons had been ejected from their longtime residence.

Sir John Johnson was not the person his father had been. He was unable to win the allegiance of large groups of American Indians. The American revolutionaries saw him as a threat, nonetheless, and in the spring of 1776, a Continental army group moved to Johnson Hall to seize the cannon and supplies of ammunition there. Johnson and his relatives escaped just hours before the militia arrived. They had a long, heartbreaking journey to Canada, where they became refugees, dependent on the British army. What neither Johnson nor the Mohawk who accompanied him realized was that this was the last time they would live in their beloved river valley.

The war had now come to the Mohawk Valley.

BURGOYNE'S PLAN

During the winter of 1776 to 1777, British General John Burgoyne drew up a detailed plan for crushing the American rebellion. Compiling maps and charts in far-off London, Burgoyne correctly perceived that New York was the key to the conflict: He who controlled the Hudson River, Lake George, and Lake Champlain would be the eventual victor. Burgoyne's plan was for three

British armies to converge on Albany and hold the entire series of waterways—including the Mohawk River—that governed New York state. There was much to recommend the plan, and King George and his war ministers gave it their approval.

Of the three armies, Burgoyne's moved the earliest. He started at Montreal, moved down Lake Champlain, and, more easily than expected, he captured Fort Ticonderoga (close to the site where Samuel de Champlain had fought the Mohawk in 1609). Albany was less than a hundred miles (160 km) away, and it seemed as if Burgoyne's plans were on the verge of success.

The second and smallest of the armies moved second. Colonel Barry St. Leger took a combined force of British regulars and American Indian warriors (many of them Mohawk) from Montreal, and hooked west-by-southwest, headed for Lake Ontario. He crossed the Handsome Lake without opposition and reached the "Great Carrying Place" between Lake Oneida and the Mohawk River before encountering opposition. St. Leger stopped at Fort Stanwix and settled down to a siege.

If the third and largest of the British armies had moved in time, the British victory might have been complete. But General William Howe, who commanded the forces occupying New York City, moved too late. Not only that, he went in the wrong direction, and instead of attacking Albany he moved on Philadelphia, where the Continental Congress was in session. The largest, most important of the armies was removed from the scene by the bad judgment of its commander. Burgoyne and St. Leger were left to fend for themselves.

SIX NATIONS AT WAR

Until the summer of 1777, Six Nations warriors had scarcely fought each other in two centuries. There had been the unfortunate clash between Mohawk at the Battle of Lake George but this had not provoked a serious break in Mohawk clans. The battles in upstate New York in 1777 proved much more severe.

In August, Molly Brant—then living at Canajoharie—saw a column of American militiamen on the south bank of the Mohawk River, marching west. Assuming that they intended to break the British siege of Fort Stanwix, Brant sent a Mohawk runner ahead with the news. Armed with this information, the British and their American Indian allies laid an ambush for the oncoming Americans, and the bloodiest battle of the Revolutionary War was fought at Oriskany, New York, on August 8, 1777.

Accounts of the battle vary in some details, but most agree that it was one of the hardiest, perhaps nastiest, of the entire war. The American militiamen sometimes found they had distant cousins

Drums along the Mohawk

Filmed in 1938, starring Henry Fonda and Claudette Colbert, *Drums along the Mohawk* came out just before the beginning of World War II, a time when many Americans were eager to see depictions of combat from earlier times. Battles with the tomahawk and musket seemed very safe compared to the fright of German tanks and planes, which were beginning to overrun large parts of Western Europe. A great coincidence of the film is that Henry Fonda was descended from a farmer who had settled in the Mohawk Valley in the 1750s. (See final chapter for present ownership of that land.)

The film was a definite improvement on most studies or treatments of the time. It accurately depicted the land struggles of Revolution-era New York state. If the film erred, it did so in favor of the American revolutionaries, usually depicted as heroic and selfless, while it showed the Native Americans as capable of all sorts of barbarity. Even so, it was one of the most influential films of the time.

on the British side. The American Indians found a host of their relatives as opponents. Oneida warriors were out in large numbers for the Americans, and Mohawk warriors were mostly there for the British. Though the two armies were not as large as those deployed on other Revolutionary War battlefields, the casualty lists were horrendous, as many as two-thirds killed or wounded on both sides. American General Herkimer fell in the battle, and his militiamen yielded the field to the British and American Indians. Even so, it was hard to name a real victor of the Battle of Oriskany.

Barbara Graymont, who wrote the most detailed history available of the Iroquois in the Revolutionary War, claimed that the

Drums was not surpassed as a wilderness epic until 1991, when *Last of the Mohicans* was released in theaters. Starring Daniel Day Lewis and Madeline Stowe, *Last of the Mohicans* depicted upstate New York in 1757, when the French and their American Indian allies laid siege to Fort William Henry, on the very site where Sir William Johnson had previously won the Battle of Lake George. Daniel Day Lewis was very successful in his role as the coonskin-cap frontier American of half European and half native ancestry. In a moving scene with Stowe, Lewis explained that his American Indian father had told him not to trust the British or the Americans, that they were a breed apart.

Filmmaking had advanced between 1938 and 1991, and so had characterizations of Native Americans. There was a scene showing the massacre of unarmed men and women as they marched from Fort William Henry, but the viewer also saw that Chief Magua's thirst for revenge came from the loss of his family. Many viewers came away from *Last of the Mohicans* as deeply moved as their grandparents had been from *Drums along the Mohawk*.

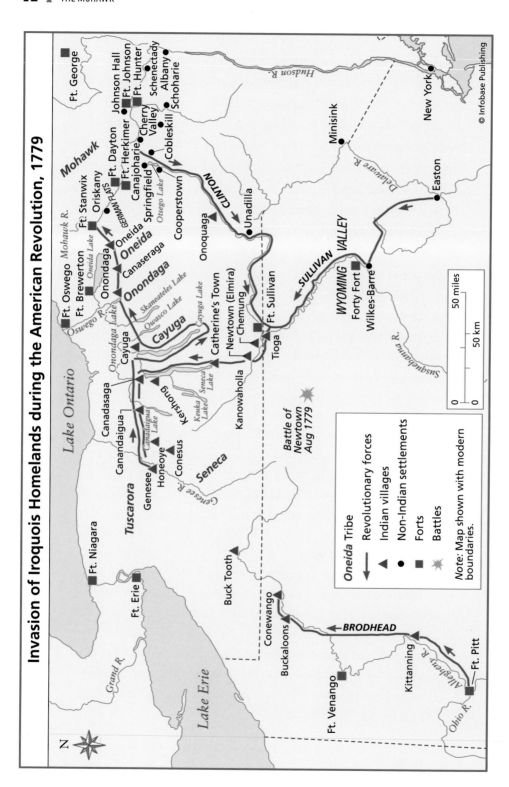

Invasion of Iroquois Homelands during the American Revolution, 1779

© Infobase Publishing

Legend

Oneida Tribe
→ Revolutionary forces
◀ Indian villages
● Non-Indian settlements
■ Forts
✳ Battles

Note: Map shown with modern boundaries.

50 miles
50 km
0
0

Battle of Newtown Aug 1779

CLINTON
SULLIVAN
WYOMING VALLEY
BRODHEAD

Mohawk had always shown a preference for short campaigns, as well as a tendency to avoid major battles, in order to preserve the lives of their warriors. After Oriskany, the British found their American Indian allies eager to depart, while the Oneida and some Tuscarora showed a willingness to continue the campaign. In the end, a clever ruse by the Americans persuaded St. Leger's army to depart. A half-witted mixed American Indian/white man known as Hans Yost staggered into the British camp, claiming that the Americans were coming, that they were as numerous as the leaves on the trees, and that they were bringing smallpox with them. This last claim was what panicked the American Indians present. Colonel St. Leger woke the next day to find his allies gone. He had no choice but to follow suit.

Only one British army remained, that of General John Burgoyne. After a short campaign involving fighting between Six Nations warriors on both sides, Burgoyne surrendered his army on October 17, 1777, at Saratoga, New York. The year of the "three sevens," as it was called, had been disastrous for the British cause.

CHERRY VALLEY AND GERMAN FLATS

Molly Brant fled the Mohawk Valley soon after the Battle of Oriskany. She and a group of loyal Mohawk went first to what is now Kingston, Ontario, and then found refuge at Fort Niagara, held by the British.

Joseph Brant was appalled by the defeats in upstate New York. He made a serious mistake in their aftermath by allying himself with Butler's Rangers, a hardcore group of American loyalists who wanted to ravage the American frontier. How many Native

(*Opposite map*) During the American Revolution, many battles took place on Native American land. Campaigning throughout the New York region destroyed Iroquois villages, hunting grounds, burned cornfields, and massacred villagers. The Six Nations, once praised for their unity, were now separated by conflict and scattered throughout North America.

Americans were present at the fierce attack on Cherry Valley, New York, is unknown, but frontier Americans blamed Joseph Brant and Colonel Walter Butler, both of whose reputations began to resemble that of the devil.

The American Indians and loyalists came back in 1780 to attack German Flats, in the very center of the Mohawk River Valley. They burned and pillaged, but whatever satisfaction they gained was short-lived, for the anger of the white settlers meant that no Mohawk would be allowed to resettle that area.

PEACE TREATIES

In 1781, the American revolutionaries won the Battle of Yorktown, where yet another British army surrendered to its former colonists. By 1782, serious negotiations were underway, and in 1783, the second Peace of Paris was signed. (The first had been in 1763.) Under its provisions, the British not only acknowledged the independence of the 13 former colonies (now states), but they indicated the new United States had claim to virtually all land east of the Mississippi River, and south of the Canadian border.

The British did nothing to assist their American Indian allies who had been so loyal to King George. The Mohawk were thus in an especially bad situation. Those few who had been neutral or friendly to the Americans were still south of the border, but the majority were either at Fort Niagara, on the Bay of Quinte (in Ontario), or outside Montreal. Previous battles and wars had taken a toll on the Mohawk, but none had left them divided in this way.

The war between the 13 fires and England was an unmitigated disaster for the Mohawk people.

Assimilate, Accommodate, or Perish

Two works of art display the divided legacy of the Mohawk in the 1780s. The first is a painting of a rather handsome Joseph Brant, with his face toward the viewer and his right arm extended. He points in the direction of the Grand River in Ontario, which he hopes will become the new home of the Six Nations. Brant has less hair in this picture than in the famous George Romney painting. The Revolutionary War had sobered him, but he still envisions great things for his people.

The second illustration is featured in the first pages of a book entitled *A Primer for the Education of Mohawk Children.* The print shows a classroom of Mohawk children who look as if they are between 5 and 10 years old. A middle-aged man whose haircut has a distinctive Mohawk look sits among them, holding out his arm as if to say that this learning—which had previously belonged to the white people—is the road forward. Published in Montreal, the

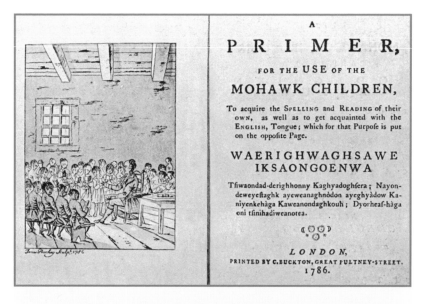

A

PRIMER,

FOR THE USE OF THE

MOHAWK CHILDREN,

To acquire the SPELLING and READING of their
own, as well as to get acquainted with the
ENGLISH, Tongue; which for that Purpose is put
on the opposite Page.

WAERIGHWAGHSAWE
IKSAONGOENWA

Tſiwaondad-derighhonny Kaghyadoghſera; Nayon-
deweyeſtaghk ayeweanaghnôdon ayeghyàdow Ka-
niyenkehàga Kaweanondaghkouh; Dyorheaſ-hàga
oni tſinihadiweanotea.

(◎◎)
◌

LONDON,

PRINTED BY C.BUCKTON, GREAT PULTNEY-STREET.
1786.

In an effort to assimilate Native American children into "mainstream" society, Native American boarding schools, run by Christian missionaries, were established. These children were forced to abandon their Native American identities and instead had to adopt European-American culture. Pictured is the title page from book, *A Primer for the Use of the Mohawk Children*.

primer was written by Daniel Claus, a son-in-law of Sir William Johnson.

Between them, these images present the dilemma faced by late nineteenth century Mohawk: to adapt, assimilate, or struggle fruitlessly against white civilization.

THE SIX NATIONS RESERVE

Joseph Brant was the best-known Mohawk of his time, and King George's government took care in its negotiations with the "loyal Mohawk." In 1784, a large land grant was established on both sides of the Grand River in eastern Ontario. Located 40 miles (65 km) west of Niagara Falls, the Grand River was a fine location, with good farmland and protection from the United States. Brant led about 1,400 Six Nations people there in 1784, about 480 of whom were Mohawk. His sister, meanwhile, had carved out a place of her own.

There was no ill will between Joseph and Molly Brant, just a desire to have their own domiciles. In the 1780s she established a much smaller reserve, principally for the Mohawk, on the Bay of Quinte, close to Kingston, Ontario. This location was less favored by nature, but the group did well there. There were still other reserves, as they are called in Canada, which had been established earlier.

Caughnawaga, meaning "place by the rapids," was renamed *Kahnawake* sometime in the nineteenth century. It had the largest population of Mohawk to be found, north or south of the border. Akwesasne, which literally straddled the U.S.-Canadian border, was founded in the 1740s. It grew rapidly, to the point that it was the number-two post. But there were other developments that influenced the Mohawk, even if they came from other members of the Six Nations.

TREATIES

In 1784, at the conclusion of the Revolutionary War, American diplomats met with Iroquois at Fort Stanwix, which was both the site of the 1777 siege and the place where in 1768 Sir William Johnson had signed away Mohawk rights to a section of their land. The negotiations of 1784 were much worse than those of 1768, for the Six Nations were now in a truly precarious position.

The 13 colonies had become the 13 states, but they were not united in a grand union yet. (The Constitution would be written three years later.) New York state diplomats held the upper hand. They forced the Six Nations people to yield much of their upstate lands, but promised that the remaining lands would be theirs for all time. This type of promise of "so long as the rivers shall run and the grass shall grow" was endemic in American Indian treaties of the time. The Oneida and Onondaga fared poorly. The Seneca, Cayuga, and Tuscarora saw their lands shrink. There is no doubt, however, that the Mohawk received the worst treatment of all. So many Mohawk had moved north of the border and were living in Canada that the white negotiators were able to brush aside any remaining claim to Mohawk land rights in the river valley.

Ten years later, in 1794, the Six Nations received a slight improvement under the terms of the (John) Jay Treaty, signed between Britain and the new United States. American and British diplomats put their signatures to a treaty that guaranteed the right of free passage for American Indians—and their goods—across the international boundary. Though it would be contested many times, the Jay Treaty became an article of faith for Northeastern Woodland Indians, especially the Mohawk.

HANDSOME LAKE

He was a Seneca, a brother of the chief Cornplanter, who made a series of treaties with President George Washington. Like many Seneca, Handsome Lake was distressed by the degradation of his community. Drunkenness abounded in reservation villages, and the Seneca, as a whole, seemed on the way to oblivion. In the summer of 1799, Handsome Lake had the first of a series of dreams in which a number of spiritual figures told him that his task was to bring new life to his people. Handsome Lake never called himself the new Deganawidah (that would have been presumptuous) but, like the Huron peacemaker, he had to work with a disability; he suffered from alcoholism.

Thanks to the visions, Handsome Lake was able to overcome his addiction to alcohol. This was the first step in making him a prophet of the "New Law" or "New Way." Handsome Lake knew enough white people, including well-intentioned Quakers, to see that his people had to make adaptations in order to survive. His new law code, which was formally inscribed many years later, made some major alterations to the Iroquois way of life. From time immemorial, the relationship between mother and daughter, and mother and granddaughter had been primary. Descent was traced matrilineally, and women were seen as the heart of the tribe. Handsome

Lake was no male chauvinist (he saw the value of women in the great chain of society) but he recognized that white people—whether army generals, store owners, or simply land-hungry farmers—were more likely to recognize and respect a system like their own, based primarily on the relationship between husband and wife. The Good Law therefore spoke of the importance of fathers and sons, and the relationship between husband and wife.

Handsome Lake died in 1815, by which time many Seneca and quite a few other Iroquois had embraced his message. His teachings spread to the Canadian Mohawk, though they never won a majority of those peoples. Handsome Lake was the first of a number of Six Nations sachems (some of them his relatives) who spoke in terms of accommodation with the white people, and adjustment to new ways of living.

MALE ROLES

By 1812, the year war began between Britain and the United States, Mohawk men and their Six Nations cousins felt much reduced in importance. A century before, they had been free agents. They roamed the great woodland areas and brought back meat to the village, where they felt honored and respected. Much of their self-esteem was based on hunting and war-making abilities, so the long period of peace was a detriment to them. When the War of 1812 began, the Mohawk were divided over whom to support. Even the Six Nations Reserve in Ontario flirted with the idea of joining the Americans, but this idea was scotched when the great resistance leader Tecumseh died at the Battle of the Thames in 1813.

Mohawk men could farm, but it did not appeal to their nature. Throughout history, farming had been the role of the women of the tribe. In the decades that followed the War of 1812, quite a few Mohawk men took up the plow, but others searched for work that would be more meaningful to them. Sometime in the nineteenth century, several Mohawk traditions began that spawned crafts or cottage industries that would support the Mohawk people.

Basket making has been a fundamental means of earning a living for the St. Regis Mohawk (Akwesasne) tribe. Their baskets have become world-renowned and have been displayed in museums. In this photograph, St. Regis Mohawk men and women are shown with P. Daly, a buyer of their baskets.

Pounded ash baskets were a Mohawk specialty. Men and women made them, and women took them to white towns and villages for sale. Mohawk craftsmanship became appreciated by white neighbors, and people often said they wanted a Mohawk basket or none at all. More in line with the traditional Mohawk way of life was the risky business of canoeing, whether on the Great Lakes or on rivers of the Far West. Almost every party of Canadian explorers had some Mohawk in their group, and several British-Canadian officers noted their preference for Mohawk canoe men. So strong was this preference that in about 1879, a number of Canadian Mohawk were recruited for paddle work in far-off Egypt during an expedition down the Nile.

Quite a few Mohawk went in the other direction, far westward. If the eastern woodland region was mostly tame farmland, the Great Plains and the Canadian prairies still offered high adventure, as David S. Blanchard describes in his dissertation on the Kahnawake Mohawk:

> The Iroquois treated our warnings with contempt when advised to be cautious in the hunting of the bison, especially when wounded; they would laugh and they killed an oxe with the stroke of an axe, and would do the same to the bisons. . . . A few days later, as two of them were hunting (they always went by twos) they met a colored bear [grizzly], which one of them wounded, the bear sprang on him, and standing on his hind feet, seized the Iroquois hugging him with his fore arms and legs.

The Mohawk hunter was badly wounded, but he was back on the hunt within six weeks. As Blanchard has it, quoting William Fenton, one of the cardinal rules of Six Nations life is that "a man never refuses when asked, and he never shows fear."

WOMEN'S ROLES

Nineteenth century transitions were a bit easier on Mohawk women. From the time of Deganawidah, they were seen as the center of Mohawk life, the keepers of the fire and home, and it was more possible to continue with this than it was for a man to continue to assert himself as a warrior and hunter. Mohawk women did have to make adjustments, however, which sometimes must have been hard on their pride. They took the pounded-ash baskets to market, and they often received the jeers or contempt of Americans or Canadians, depending on where they lived. Some Mohawk women, however, were viewed with great respect by their white neighbors. One of the most poignant examples was described by Lawrence Hauptman in *Seven Generations of Iroquois Leadership*.

> To the white people of central New York who frequently read about her in local newspapers or saw her on the streets, 'Aunt

Dinah' was a non-threatening loyal American, a kind, dignified old Indian lady who bridged the 'uncivilized' and 'antiquated' world of the reservation down the road with that of modern industrial Syracuse. . . . Throughout much of her exceptionally long life she was to be seen as an exceptionally hard-working entrepreneur off the reservation. Until well past the age of ninety, she walked the three-and-a-half miles nearly every morning from the Onondaga Reservation to the downtown area of Syracuse to sell her Indian baskets and pots.

By mid-century, many Americans felt that the Native Americans were a relic that must surely melt away with the coming of the twentieth century. Happily, there were a few white Americans who saw something special, even precious, about Native American traditions.

The Mohawk on the Performance Circuit

One of the least-remembered aspects of Mohawk life is the many performances enacted by tribe members during the nineteenth century. At a time when many people believed that the Native Americans would disappear, performance groups like Buffalo Bill Cody's Wild West Show became ever more popular. Who wouldn't want to see a people and way of life that might soon be gone?

There may have been earlier performances, but the ones conducted in 1860 in Canada for Albert, the Prince of Wales, represented a turning point. Prince Albert was so entranced by the Canadian Mohawk dancers and by the canoe men that he invited a small group of them to come to England the next year to perform before his mother, Queen Victoria. By then, the memory of the four "Indian Kings" of 1710 had faded, and Londoners (and later Parisians) were thrilled to see these American Indian

HENRY LEWIS MORGAN

Born in upstate New York, Morgan was a college student when he first became interested in the Six Nations. In his twenties he "played Indian," establishing so-called native societies with his white friends, and acting enamored of the Native American lifestyle. In his thirties, Morgan became a serious scholar, and his *League of the Iroquois,* published in 1851, is considered one of the marvels of early ethnohistory. He writes:

> Among the Indian nations whose ancient seats were within the limits of our republic, the Iroquois have long continued to occupy the most conspicuous position. They achieved for themselves a more remarkable civil organization, and acquired

performances, complete with social dances as well as rituals. Some were completely authentic Mohawk dances, but others had been enhanced by borrowing from Western tribes such as the Sioux. This first round of visits was only the beginning.

Kahnawake Reserve, just outside of Montreal, provided the largest number of dancers and performers, some of whom went to Europe in addition to touring sections of the eastern United States in the last decades of the nineteenth century. No one Mohawk man or woman stands out, but hundreds made decent livings on the road, performing in New England towns and villages. They also managed to keep the idea of the Mohawk alive to a generation of whites who had never seen an actual longhouse, or felt any insecurity about American Indians on the border.

The performance circuit gave Mohawk women the chance to demonstrate their skills, too. No figures exist for how many Mohawk women performed, but it was enough to build their reputation in a time when the American Indian seemed fated to disappear.

a higher degree of influence, than any other race of Indian lineage, except those of Mexico and Peru. In the drama of European colonization, they stood, for nearly two centuries, with an unshaken front, against the devastations of war, the blighting influence of foreign intercourse and the still more fatal encroachments of a restless and advancing border population.

Many historians and ethnologists today would dispute certain points, but most would agree that Morgan's *League of the Iroquois* was an outstanding achievement. From him, we learn of sachems' names, seasonal rituals, and even the native names for towns and cities of today. Today's reader finds that the Mohawk name for Albany was *Ska-neh-ta-die* ("beyond the openings"), that Rochester was called *Ga-skun-sa-go* ("under the falls"), and that the traditional spelling for Canajoharie was *Ga-no-jo-har-la* ("washing the basin"). If Morgan had not done this difficult work of translation and interpretation, much of this might have been lost forever.

CHANGES IN CANADA

By 1867, the year Canada attained "Dominion" status, there were considerably more Mohawk north of the international boundary than to its south. The Canadian Mohawk resented a series of changes in Canadian law.

In 1869, Canada passed its first comprehensive act involving the fate of the American Indians. There were some positive aspects to the legislation, but there was a marked tendency toward changing the lives of the tribal peoples to resemble those of white peoples. One of the most important aspects, and from the Mohawk point of view, one of the most destructive, was that descent in Canada was always to be traced through the male line. From time immemorial, the Mohawk had traced descent through the mother and grandmother, assigning clan status based on the clan of one's female ancestors. Many Mohawk families continued to do this in secret. Those who fully accepted the new Canadian law were sometimes estranged from relatives who did not.

CENSUS OF 1890

The U.S. Census of 1890 revealed that persons who self-identified as American Indians had dropped to a very low point, about a quarter of a million in a total national population of 70 million. Interested in knowing more about the Six Nations, the Census sponsored a special report that was published two years later. The bulletin, entitled *The Six Nations of New York,* provided more detailed evidence than had ever been seen on an American Indian group. The reader learned that the Six Nations had never disappeared from New York state, and that they lived on six major reservations: Onondaga, Tonawanda, Allegany, Cattaraugus, Tuscarora, and St. Regis, with a total population of 5,133 persons.

After the wars, the Mohawk spread throughout New York State and southeastern Canada. In 1888, the Mohawk tribe, who had maintained their traditions and ceremonies, recaptured their place as the "elder brother" of the Iroquois Confederacy. Many tribal members showed their pride by wearing native clothing, like these St. Regis Indian Show people.

One of the most interesting categories was that of occupations. At the St. Regis Reservation (also called Akwesasne) there were: 177 basket makers, 9 bead workers, 1 maker of snowshoes, 4 carpenters, 1 clerk, 5 domestic laborers, 3 engineers, 113 farmers, 10 hunters and fishermen, 6 gardeners, 3 guides, 1 housekeeper, 48 laborers, 2 lumbermen, 2 mechanics, 2 merchants, 1 music teacher, 1 musician, 1 preacher, and 9 people listed as "show people." By contrast, the other five reservations listed had only 5 basket makers and 4 show people combined. These were occupations that the Mohawk had carved for themselves.

Another important category was that of domestic animals. The St. Regis Mohawk had 266 horses, 138 swine, 9,292 domestic fowls, and 472 head of cattle. One of the most important verbal descriptions of the St. Regis Mohawk concerned their being separated by the U.S.-Canadian border.

> The boundary line established by the treaty of Washington [1871] about equally divides the population of the American and Canadian members of the St. Regis nation. The house of John J. Deer, 'Running Deer,' known as the 'International Hotel,' is bisected diagonally by the boundary line. It also cuts off one of the rooms of John Papineau's house.

CENTURY'S END

As the nineteenth century neared its end, the Mohawk were as divided as ever, both by the international border and the different traditions that had developed. There were ardent followers of Handsome Lake's new religion, and there were quiet devotees of the older ways. There were Mohawk who embraced the writings of whites such as Lewis Henry Morgan, whose *League of the Iroquois* became something of a classic, and others who rejected the efforts of white people to understand them.

Iron, Steel, and Standing Arrow

A new line of work opened for Mohawk men toward the end of the nineteenth century. The new endeavor was described by the social critic Edmund Wilson in *Apologies to the Iroquois*.

> In the erection of steel structures, whether bridge or building, there are three main divisions of workers—raising gangs, fitting-up gangs, and riveting gangs. The steel comes to a job already cut and built into various kinds of columns and beams and girders; the columns are the perpendicular pieces and the beams and girders are the horizontal ones. . . . Using a crane or a derrick, the men in the raising gang hoist the pieces up and set them in position and join them by running bolts through a few of the holes in them: these bolts are temporary. Then the men in the fitting-up gang come along; they are divided into plumbers and bolters.

All the tasks were difficult, but that of the riveter was the most frightening of all. He had to keep his balance while blasting metal through steel, making sure that the bridge or skyscraper held. Who would want to do this work?

The Mohawk.

BRIDGES OVER THE ST. LAWRENCE

To the best of our knowledge, the Mohawk interest in high iron and steel commenced around 1887, when a railroad company built a bridge across the St. Lawrence River, just outside Montreal. A handful of Mohawk men went to look, and came away convinced they could do this work better than their white counterparts. Whether the Mohawk actually experienced less fear working at such dizzying heights, or whether they simply pretended to be fearless, remains subject to debate.

That first bridge project led to others, and by about 1900 there were crews of Mohawk men working on many of the bridges and high-rise buildings of Canada. Most of it went very well, but there was a great disaster in September 1907, when the famed Quebec cantilever bridge collapsed, killing about 70 men, most of them Kahnawake Mohawk. As David S. Blanchard described it, there was only one telephone on the Kahnawake Reserve, and whole families had to wait for days by that phone to receive the news, much of it bad. The women of Kahnawake gathered to announce that from then on, gangs of Mohawk workers had to split up so that there would never be a large number on any one iron or steel job. (That policy remains in place today.)

Mohawk men from Kahnawake and Akwesasne continued to flock to the trade, however, both for its excitement and the good money. For the first time in a century, Mohawk men had an adventurous way of making a living, one that called to mind the daring actions of their ancestors. There was a difficult by-product, in that many Mohawk households were deprived of husbands and fathers

The Mohawk labored as steel workers on nearly all of the monumental structures in New York, including the Empire State Building, the Chrysler Building, the George Washington Bridge, the World Trade Center, the Verrazzano Bridge, the Triborough Bridge, the Pulaski Skyway, and the West Side Highway. They have been called some of the greatest iron workers in the world.

for long periods of time. To overcome this, some Mohawk women agreed to be ready to pick up and move long distances. As Joseph Mitchell and Edmund Wilson expressed it:

> It is not unusual for a family to lock up its house, leave the key with a neighbor, get into an automobile, and go away for years. There are colonies of Caughnawagas in Brooklyn, Buffalo, and Detroit. The biggest colony is in Brooklyn, out in the North Gowanus neighborhood. It was started in the late twenties; there are approximately four hundred men, women, and children in it.

The Brooklyn group became so large that a local Presbyterian church devoted itself to their pastoral care. Reverend David Munroe Cory learned the Mohawk language and specialized with his Mohawk congregants.

Munroe's church became the center of American Indian life in Brooklyn. His congregants looked to him with admiration, for here was a multi-faceted man, one who could preach in their language, who believed in a socialist worldview, and who even participated in the annual jump into the Atlantic every New Year's Day. He did not come to his work by accident; his father had written a number of novels, many centered around American Indian life.

THE ROARING TWENTIES

In the 1920s, some American Indians prospered in the growing economy. The community of Akwesasne was among them, thanks to a burgeoning trade in liquor. It was during this decade that a Mohawk named Paul Diabo made a test case of the famous Jay Treaty of 1794.

Diabo was a Kahnawake ironworker who frequently commuted between Canada and the United States. In 1925, New York police arrested him in Albany and charged him with illegal entry. Diabo took his case to the courts, and it eventually rose to the Supreme Court, which handed down its decision in 1927. According to Judge Buffington, Diabo had a spotless personal record, and had been engaged in ironwork—and commuting between Kahnawake and New York—for over a decade. The judge used both the Jay Treaty provision ("It shall at all times be free to his majesty's subjects, and to the citizens of the United States, and also to the Indians dwelling on either side of the said boundary line") and the ruling of Chief Justice John Marshall in 1832 ("They [the Indian groups] may, more correctly, perhaps, be denominated domestic dependent nations"). Judge Buffington found for the defendant, a major victory for the Mohawk in Canada and the United States.

THE NEW DEAL

Franklin D. Roosevelt swept into office in 1933, determined to combat the crippling effects of the Great Depression. In just his

War and Citizenship

As late as 1920, it was still questionable whether American Indians were citizens of the United States. Many Iroquois, Mohawk included, resisted the idea because they traced their lineage to a time of national sovereignty. According to them, the many treaties between Native peoples and the U.S. government would no longer be valid if they became full citizens. War provided the answer to this dilemma.

Canadian Mohawk joined the British forces early in World War I. Many of their American brethren followed when the United States entered in 1917. At least 10,000 American Indians served in the U.S. Army during the year and a half of fighting. When the Great War ended, there was a strong movement to make them citizens. American women won the right to vote, in part due to their work during the war. It seemed only natural that American Indians should benefit, too.

In 1924, Congress passed the Indian Citizenship Act without much resistance or fanfare. Mohawk groups were in the forefront of those who opposed it, but the citizenship act was an idea whose time had come. American Indians could vote in national elections for the first time.

World War II was a different story. Because of the citizenship act, all able-bodied Native American men were now subject to the draft. Many resisted, leading to some ugly scenes on reservations, with local white people calling the American Indians unpatriotic. As a way of sidestepping the matter, a handful of Six Nations chiefs went to Washington, D.C., in the summer of 1942 to make their own formal declaration of war against Hitler and his allies. The deed was done on July 1, 1942, with Vice President Henry Wallace standing next to Onondaga Chief Jesse Lyons. But some damage had already been wrought. For years after, many white Americans questioned the patriotism of American Indians, believing they had not done their part in the war effort.

first 100 days in office, FDR pushed through a number of programs. One that had to wait until 1934 was the Indian Reorganization Act. Written and implemented by secretary John Collier, the act was designed to halt and reverse the effects of the Allotment Act.

The Allotment Act of 1887 had been drafted with all good intentions, but it had led to the loss of millions of acres of land, snapped up by speculators who understood the rules better than the American Indians. The Mohawk had not really lost under Allotment, because they had so little land remaining in the United States. Had Canada put through a similar act, they would have been in serious trouble. They and their Six Nations cousins were therefore mostly in the role of spectators as Collier and an idealistic group of bureaucrats tried to change course for the American Indian.

The Indian Reorganization Act (IRA), written in 1934, was the most controversial aspect of the New Deal as it pertained to American Indians. Collier wanted to enhance the status of American Indians, including the Iroquois, but he did not make any personal outreach to those who lived in upstate New York. Even though his idea of granting voting rights to Six Nations women was progressive for the time, many Mohawk resented it as an intrusion into their lives. They said that Mohawk women had always possessed political influence but that they used it behind the scenes. The St. Regis Reservation rejected the IRA by the lopsided margin of 237 opposed, 46 in favor, and 517 choosing not to vote. Even though Collier had the authority to move ahead with a tribal reorganization, he decided against it.

FDR did not have a soft spot for Native Americans in general. His record was about the same toward them as toward African Americans. The New Deal years offered hope to many American Indians, however, and when FDR died of natural causes in 1945, many mourned the loss.

POSTWAR YEARS

Collier resigned as Commissioner of Indian Affairs in 1945, and for the next several years there was a moratorium on new government programs and on plans to change the American Indians. What came next was a big surprise; proponents called it Termination.

Dillon S. Myer was coordinator of the internment of Japanese-Americans during World War II, and he also became the leading official for the policy of Termination, officially endorsed by Congress in 1953. Unlike Allotment (intended to turn American Indians into family farmers) and the New Deal (intended to spur American Indian participation in white life), Termination was intended to put an end to American Indian reservations and the legal sovereignty that protected them. American Indians were to give up their "Indianness" and become full members of white society.

ST. LAWRENCE SEAWAY

Termination became U.S. policy under President Dwight D. Eisenhower. The president was not heavily involved in the process; his interests in foreign policy were stronger than domestic ones. During the 1950s, President Eisenhower moved ahead with a major construction project meant to widen and deepen the St. Lawrence River so oceangoing ships could make their way to Chicago and Detroit. The seaway was a joint project of the U.S. and Canadian governments, and no one thought to ask the Mohawk or their Six Nations cousins whether it was a good idea or not.

Quite a few Mohawk were in favor of the seaway project when it was announced, for it was clear that major companies like ALCOA and General Motors would build new plants in the St. Lawrence region. Jobs were expected, and many Mohawk signaled their acceptance of the program. Once the seaway was completed in 1958, it was apparent that some parts of the program were detrimental to Mohawk life. Kahnawake's original name was Caughnawaga ("place by the rapids") but the seaway cut through the marshy, swampy soil, making Kahnawake a backwater instead of a thriving place by the water. The high technology industrial plants did come to the area, especially to the land near Akwesasne, but the American companies hired few Mohawk workers. Even so, many Mohawk would have accepted the situation except for the environmental degradation that ensued.

Kahnawake was no longer a "place by the rapids" and Akwesasne was no longer a "place where the partridge drums." Heavy metals seeped into the soil around the St. Lawrence, both contaminating the local fish supply and introducing chemicals into the area where Akwesasne farmers had dairy cattle.

KINZUA DAM

At the same time as Mohawk were facing the St. Lawrence Seaway, their Seneca and Tuscarora cousins were imposed upon by the Kinzua Dam in western New York and Pennsylvania. Another brainchild of the developer Robert Moses, the Kinzua Dam was intended to provide cheap electricity to millions of people, but it needed land that had belonged to Six Nations people for many generations.

For the first time in decades, the Seneca and Tuscarora became visible to their white neighbors. In part, this was because protestors had adopted American Indian-style dress (that resembled Plains Indians) and also because the national media picked up on the story. The number of white Americans who sympathized with the American Indians was hard to determine, but at a time when the United States was locked in the Cold War with the Soviet Union, many whites looked upon the Seneca and Tuscarora as backward people, standing in the way of progress. Even the election of the liberal John F. Kennedy to the U.S. presidency did not alter the situation. The Kinzua Dam went ahead.

OCCUPATION OF THE VALLEY

It was around this time—the mid 1950s—that a tiny group of Mohawk began to resettle in the river valley their ancestors had possessed for hundreds of years. Social critic Edmund Wilson

In 1957, Chief Standing Arrow (*standing, left*) and his Mohawk follow-ers established a settlement on some land on the Schoharie Creek, near Amsterdam, New York. The chief insisted that the Treaty of Fort Stanwix had assigned the land to the Mohawk in 1784. The conflict was never settled.

described his encounter with Chief Standing Arrow in *Apologies to the Iroquois,* published in 1959:

> Standing Arrow commenced our interview by getting a little tough—understandably in view of the fact that on first meet-ing him I had challenged him rather sharply; but he soon began exerting charm. Though he had a slight cast in one eye, his features were rather fine and reminded me of portraits of the youthful Napoleon. He had also, as I could see, some of the qualities of the Mussolinian spellbinder.

Wilson went on to describe Standing Arrow's oratorical methods, which reminded him of the great speeches made by Six Nations chiefs and sachems over the course of centuries.

He used gestures, as he spoke, of a kind that rather surprised me on the part of an Indian, gestures which I thought might perhaps have been picked up from the Canadian French and which seemed to show experience in public speaking. When I talked later to another Mohawk—not one of Standing Arrow's followers—he answered, 'he's got a touch of the hypnotist. People go to him prejudiced against him and come away completely convinced.' Another Mohawk, who disapproved of him, told me that his eloquence in English—of which his command was imperfect—was nothing to his eloquence in Mohawk. 'When he talks to me, as long as he's there, I can't disagree with anything he says.'

Standing Arrow showed Edmund Wilson all sorts of documents about the 1784 and 1794 treaties between the Iroquois and the United States, all purporting to show that the Mohawk River Valley belonged to his people. Wilson was never entirely convinced of the paper trail, but his conversations with Standing Arrow persuaded him that he had been entirely wrong to think that Native Americans were a vanished people, belonging only in museums and movies.

Native Image /
Native Reality
at the End of the
Twentieth Century

Three images serve to illuminate stereotypes of the Mohawk in the late twentieth century. The first is of a compliant Native American who seldom says more than "me red skin, you pale face." The second is of a wise, compassionate tribal leader who knows that his people are in trouble, both because of environmental change and the arrival of the white peoples. The third is a rather vicious, but strangely compelling, portrayal of a Native American gone mad with the desire for revenge.

TONTO

Americans of all ethnic backgrounds who came of age in the 1950s grew up with a television series called *The Lone Ranger*. Coming to the screen in the mid 1950s, when television was still in its infancy, the Lone Ranger epitomized a guts-and-glory approach to American life, especially in the Far West. The lead was played by Clayton

Moore, whose face was never fully revealed to the camera. His back-up, or sidekick, was played by Jay Silverheels, a Mohawk from the Grand River Reserve in Ontario (founded by Joseph Brant in 1784).

Jay Silverheels (*right*) was born as Harold J. Smith on a reservation to a Mohawk chief. He first appeared in films simply as "Indian." Although he was still playing the stereotypical role in the television series *The Lone Ranger,* his role as Tonto would bring him fame.

Few television viewers realized that Jay Silverheels was Mohawk (or that his father was the most decorated American Indian in the Canadian Army during World War I), but they knew he was American Indian, and he seemed to personify a type of submissive behavior that reflected the stereotypes of the time. The 1950s, after all, were a time when the official U.S. government policy toward the American Indians was known as Termination.

Silverheels died in Hollywood in March 1980. His *New York Times* obituary noted that he was the first American Indian to have his own star on Hollywood Boulevard.

THE LATE SIXTIES

It is well known that the 1960s were a turbulent time in the world of social movements, but the role played by American Indians is less visible than that of African Americans. American Indians were slow to take up the banner of "Red Power," as it was called, but as they witnessed the success of movements like those led by Martin Luther King, Jr., they hungered for one of their own. Two pivotal years, 1968 and 1969, witnessed the appearance of a new image of American Indians, both on the screen and in person.

The Mohawk community at Akwesasne—split by the international border—had become increasingly restive during the 1960s. After weeks of planning, on December 18, 1968, about 100 Mohawk seized the International Bridge, which ran across the St. Lawrence with a stop-off at Cornwall Island.

The Mohawk were led by Mike Mitchell, a college student in his twenties who had been inspired by one of his teachers, Ernest Benedict. As the Mohawk placed 25 cars in the way of traffic—effectively closing the bridge—Mitchell led his fellow protestors in a series of chants, with slogans such as, "We don't want to be a Canadian citizen," "We don't want to be an American citizen," and, most powerful of all, "This is Indian land."

Wearing the uniform of a St. Regis lacrosse player, Mitchell held the stage. (His actions were showcased in the film *This is*

Indian Land, released in 1969.) First dozens, then literally hundreds of Canadian police arrived, some from the town of Cornwall and some from the province of Ontario. Conscious that their every move was being videotaped, the officers were gentle at first, claiming they would listen to the protestors' complaints. Then, after an hour or two, their attitudes turned frosty. Believing that Mitchell was too young and impassioned, they turned to his former teacher, Ernest Benedict, a 48-year-old Mohawk who had spent years studying and teaching traditional Mohawk ways.

The police asked Benedict to get his people to remove the vehicles and depart peacefully. "I cannot order them," Benedict replied. The most he could do was stand on top of one of the vehicles and speak to his people in Mohawk. He said that the policemen were becoming angry, and that this was the appropriate time to cultivate the good will of those who would watch these actions on television. Some protestors agreed and planned to depart, but others resisted. Several hours after the occupation began, the police began arresting men and women; 47 went to jail. Mitchell called out, "See you guys in Disneyland," as he went into the police cruiser.

The day ended without significant violence. In practical terms, it was a victory for the police, but in public relations it was a win for the Mohawk, who had shown that they could demonstrate forcefully, yet peacefully. They did not know that a bigger confrontation was about to take place.

In the weeks that followed the International Bridge occupation, some of Benedict's students decided to launch a new type of periodical, one devoted entirely to aboriginal or indigenous peoples, regardless of where they lived. *Akwesasne Notes* began as a rather crude type of mimeograph production because of budget constraints. It grew in size and elegance, eventually reaching more than 100,000 subscribers around the globe. This did not mean that the lives of the Mohawk became any easier, just that Akwesasne became well known to millions of people. Activists from many nations began to congregate there.

RICHARD OAKES

Ten months later, a Mohawk from Akwesasne named Richard
Oakes became the spokesman for another, longer occupation. On

Due to the 19-month standoff in which a group of Native Americans seized
Alcatraz Island and demanded reparations for broken treaties and land that
was taken away from them, President Richard Nixon rescinded the Indian
termination policy. The occupation also played a role in the return of land to
the Taos, Yakima, Navajo, and Washhoe tribes.

November 10, 1969, he jumped off a cruise boat to swim 250 yards (230 m) in the freezing waters of San Francisco Bay to reach Alcatraz Island. (The former federal penitentiary had closed in 1963.) Though he and a handful of followers were brought back to San Francisco by the Coast Guard, Oakes had shown the way for his fellow American Indian activists. On November 20, they seized the island, claiming it belonged to American Indians of all nations.

Oakes was a superb spokesman for the movement. People watching him on television found him charismatic, even overwhelming. In an era that admired the solitary male performing

Acting and Real Life

Jay Silverheels, who played "Tonto," died in Hollywood in March 1980. The *New York Times* obituary noted that he was the first Native American to have his own star on Hollywood Boulevard. Almost a decade passed before a new crop of Native American actors—some connected with the Six Nations of Iroquois—came to the silver screen.

In the autumn of 1990, *Dances with Wolves* was released, and some observers say that the portrayal of Native American themes has been different ever since. Graham Greene, an Oneida born in upstate New York, played Kicking Bird, a gentle, wise, middle-aged sachem concerned about the future of his people. Though *Dances with Wolves* had some of the obligatory violence (tomahawks and rifles) associated with films about Native Americans, the discriminating viewer saw a fuller, rounded portrait of the Sioux Indians on the Great Plains. For a better look at the Eastern Woodland Indians, he or she had to wait until *Last of the Mohicans* was released in 1991.

Filmed in the Great Smoky Mountains of North Carolina, *Last of the Mohicans* successfully brought to life the hills, valleys, and rugged peaks of upstate New York in the colonial heroic acts, Oakes became a symbol of American Indian resistance. Unfortunately, Oakes did less well with his fellows on the island. They were weary of his leadership.

The Alcatraz story did not end well for the American Indians of all nations, nor for Richard Oakes, who played so dramatic a role. In the first weeks, Oakes was not only the spokesman for the occupation, but he also enjoyed a cult-like following among white Americans and American Indians alike. Some said that with his unruly hair and natural charisma, he seemed like another Marlon Brando or James Dean.

period. The protagonist was mixed race, who knew a good deal of both the Anglo-Americans and of his adopted tribe, but the show was stolen by Magua, a Huron Indian bent on revenge against the British colonel who had killed members of his family. Magua was a throwback, in some ways, echoing the violence and brutality of earlier stereotypical depictions of Native Americans, but his role was so convincingly played by the full-blooded Cherokee Wes Studi that he became the anti-hero of the film. To complete the synchronicity, the protagonist's father was played by the American Indian activist Russell Means, who had taken sanctuary among the Six Nations some years earlier.

The beginning of the twenty-first century saw several portrayals of the Mohawk and other Six Nations people, in more modern circumstances. *Frozen River,* released in the summer of 2008, showed the painful, sometimes desperate choices made by two women that smuggled illegal immigrants across the U.S.-Canadian border, with much of the action taking place in and around the Akwesasne reserve. One can argue that American cinema still does not have many Native American actors, but it is clear that those actors who "make it" (Jay Silverheels paved the way) are obtaining better, more convincing roles all the time.

About seven weeks into the occupation, Oakes's stepdaughter died from injuries sustained in a three-floor fall. The former prison was notoriously dangerous, but some people suspected her death was not accidental but a sharp warning to Oakes, who had become unpopular with many of his fellows on the island. Whichever the case, Oakes left Alcatraz in the spring of 1970, but his presence as a leader—and as an Akwesasne Mohawk—brought attention to Mohawk everywhere. Some of his fellow activists hung on for another year. Oakes was badly wounded in a San Francisco bar fight that same year, and then died at the hands of a park ranger during a heated argument in 1972.

A number of Mohawk also participated in the Trail of Broken Treaties, a caravan that took a series of broken promises outlined in documents from the federal government and drove to Washington, D.C., in 1972. They, too, did not accomplish their goal, and American Indian activism seemed nearly broken in the mid 1970s. That did not mean they had given up; rather, they were about to change their tactics.

U.S.-CANADIAN POLITICS

The late 1970s witnessed a strong conservative reaction, both in Canada and the United States, to the different movements of American Indians, African Americans, gays and lesbians, and others. Canada continued to pursue a middle-of-the-road policy, but the United States found a reactionary leader in Ronald Wilson Reagan, elected in November 1980.

Handsome, charming, and blessed with a wonderful voice, Reagan seemed to personify the desire among some to turn the clock back to the 1950s, or even earlier. A Hollywood movie star in the 1930s and 1940s, he had become the number-one spokesman for the General Electric Company in the 1950s, and therefore was the perfect pitch man for a white, middle-class American audience. He was quite *imperfect* at reaching Native American audiences.

To be fair, neither Lyndon B. Johnson, Richard M. Nixon, nor Jimmy Carter had been especially kind to Native Americans in their policies. The difference was that former actor Ronald Reagan looked and acted like a cowboy, an image that resonated poorly with many American Indians. His policies were not directly anti-American Indian, but they were anti-environment, at least in the eyes of many critics. Reagan opened sections of the country's national parks to logging companies, and he showed little, if any, concern over the salmon fishing in the Pacific Northwest. So far as Reagan knew, the Mohawk and their Six Nations cousins were practically invisible. Those who remembered the painful fight over the St. Lawrence Seaway and the Kinzua Dam felt that Reagan had indeed turned back the clock to the days of Eisenhower.

Reagan retired in 1989. In the last year of his presidency, Reagan had signed a bill that had momentous consequences for American Indians around the United States. Legalized gambling was about to come to the reservations.

Mohawk People in the New Century

In *Life and Death in Mohawk Country,* historian Bruce E. Johansen wrote the following passage about the upper St. Lawrence River Valley, where the Mohawk communities of Akwesasne, Kahnawake, and Kanataske were located:

> In the space of two generations, this land of natural wonders has become a place where you cannot eat the fish or game. In some places, you cannot drink the water, and in others people have been told not to till the soil. In place of a sustaining river to which Mohawks still offer thanksgiving prayers, late twentieth-century capitalism has offered them incinerators and dumps for medical waste.

When the United States and Canada created the St. Lawrence Seaway in the 1950s, the project was touted as something that would make everyone's lives better. Ships would move more

Mohawk Population Figures

Akwesasne: 10,680 persons on the reservation and 1,788 off, for a total of 12,468

Kahnawake: 7,225 persons on the reserve, 1,861 off, for a total of 9,086

Six Nations, Brantford, Ontario: 5,013 persons on the reserve, 5,029 off, for a total of 10,042

Tyendinega: 1,944 persons on the reserve, 5,325 off, for a total of 7,269

Kanesatake: 1,338 persons on the reserve, 631 off, for a total of 1,969

Total: 40,834

Source: 2000 U.S. Census and Canadian Census
Note: These figures are accurate as of the 2000 census, but may not include all Mohawk, as there are small, clustered groups that sometimes are not counted in national censuses.

easily and rapidly, goods would move from the Atlantic to the Great Lakes, and Canadians and Americans alike would enjoy the benefits of new hydroelectric power plants. No one consulted the Mohawk peoples.

By the twenty-first century, stories of environmental degradation were commonplace, but when the first news of toxic waste in the St. Lawrence reached the newspapers in the 1980s, people were horrified. They had not counted on the local industrial plants—hydroelectric, automobile, and aluminum manufacturing—having such an impact on the St. Lawrence area. Today, most people understand the problem in two words: heavy metals.

ALCOA and General Motors were the two biggest offenders. Their plants, built in the early 1960s, were right upstream from the Mohawk reserve of Akwesasne. Mohawk communities complained of seeing and smelling the fumes from the plants, but much worse was the harm that toxic waste did to fish and farming areas. All sorts of illnesses and diseases sprang up at Akwesasne, both in the human and animal populations.

By the late 1980s, the area was in a very bad way, with soaring unemployment and major public health problems, including a great increase in the number of people with diabetes. Into this confused and painful situation came the offer of money from big casinos.

LEGALIZATION

The American Indian Act of 1988 legalized casino gambling on virtually all reservations in the United States. Akwesasne had already been a major smuggling area, with the biggest profits being made from transporting cigarettes across the border. Now there was a new game in town, with much larger dollar signs. Half a dozen casinos appeared between 1988 and 1990, most of them on US Route 37, which runs through the northern section of the reservation.

The new casinos pitted brothers against brothers, sisters against sisters, and old allies who found themselves on separate sides of the fence. This was especially apparent in the case of Mike Mitchell and Francis Boots. Both in their late forties, they had been among the leaders of the bridge blockade in December 1968. They were practically neighbors on Cornwall Island in the middle of the St. Lawrence, but they were deeply divided on the casino issue. Mitchell saw the casinos as selling out the American Indian tradition while Boots hailed them as job creators for the Mohawk people. The conflict between the former allies first became apparent publicly when *National Geographic* magazine ran a special essay on the U.S.-Canadian border, entitled "Common Ground, Different Dreams."

The essay noted that southern Canada received roughly twice the amount of airborne pollutants from the United States than vice-versa, and it displayed some of the other tensions that could be seen along the border between the two countries. But nowhere were the tensions worse than in Akwesasne. Mitchell expressed his desire for the Mohawk population to produce more doctors, lawyers, and other professional types, while Boots said he did not recognize the U.S.-Canada border and that Mohawk leaders like Mitchell were way behind the times. This exchange was just the beginning of the dispute.

THE WARRIORS

Sometime during the late 1970s, a new group of militant Mohawk had emerged. Naming themselves the "Warriors of the Mohawk Nation," or simply "the Warriors," this group was composed largely of men in their thirties and forties. Some of them were Vietnam War veterans; others were hunters, fishermen, or both. Virtually all were experts in the use of firearms. During the late 1980s, the Warriors acquired a large arsenal, generally from Canadian sources, and brought the guns to the U.S. side of the border. Complicating matters, one or two Warrior leaders had close personal relationships with New York governor Mario Cuomo, who tended to take them at their word. When Akwesasne became enmeshed in conflict in the spring of 1990, the New York state police and the famed Royal Canadian Mounted Police both tried to stay out of the matter.

In March and April 1990, about 300 Mohawk opposed to casino gambling began a series of blockades on Route 37, preventing non-Indians from coming north to gamble at the numerous casinos. The anti-gambling faction was made up of about equal numbers of men and women, and there were some teenagers in their midst. They were naturally more appealing than their opponents, the heavily-armed Warriors, who sometimes wore masks to conceal their identities.

Most anti-gambling Mohawk believed that the New York state police would intervene, allowing for a cooling-off period. That did

In 1990, the first of several conflicts in the late twentieth century between the Canadian government and Native Americans erupted in violence. Kanesatake Mohawk protested Oka, Quebec's plans to expand the village's 9-hole golf course to 18 holes on Mohawk burial grounds, and one police officer was killed. Pictured are three members of the Mohawk Warriors at the main roadblock on the highway.

not happen, however, and in April things became extremely tense. Doug George, editor of *Akwesasne Notes* and a gambling opponent, noted some of the very tense occurrences:

April 15   Warriors fire more than 100 rounds near barricades

April 19   Warrior gunfire injures woman at barricade

April 21   Warriors fire into barricades

These and other conflicts had everyone on edge. Drive-by shootings were a common event, though no one was killed. Many houses went up in flames, and people began to flee the reservation. The big blow-up came on May 1, when a Warrior group attacked Doug George's home, spraying bullets and killing one man. That same night, another Mohawk man who had not joined either side was killed in the woods.

The New York state police finally intervened. When they first arrived, the police looked extremely nervous. They were there in great number, but the Mohawk Warriors had better firepower and were expert shots. The police separated the two sides and pulled down the barricades erected by the anti-gambling Mohawk group, only to put up some of their own. A tense, chilly truce descended on the reservation.

At this point, the rest of the United States might have started to pay attention to what was going on in Akwasasne, but then something bigger filled their minds. The Persian Gulf War began in August 1990 between a U.S.-led United Nations coalition and Saddam Hussein's Iraq. Almost 2 million Americans mobilized for the conflict. Suddenly, firefights between Mohawk near the Canadian border did not seem as important, unless one lived in that area. Canadian radio and television (the Internet was in its infancy) picked up the Akwesasne story instead, and the two related ones: the conflicts at Kahnawake and Kanesatake.

CONFLICT OVER THE OKA GOLF COURSE

Mohawk had been living at the confluence of the Ottawa and St. Lawrence rivers for 260 years when a conflict blew up over a golf course. Oka is a prosperous suburb of Montreal that was looking to expand its golf course from 9 links to 18. Kanesatake (the Native American settlement there, dating back to 1712) was opposed both because the golf course would swallow 30 acres

Tracey Deer: Mohawk Filmmaker

Tracey Deer was a teenager when her family fled Kahnawake during the crisis of 1990. For the rest of her life, she remembered the episode in which stones were thrown by their neighbors.

Born and raised in Kahnawake, Deer went to Queen of Angels academy for girls in Montreal. This education allowed her a better, bigger vision of the outside world. After graduating from Dartmouth College with a degree in filmmaking, she went into business for herself, producing acclaimed films such as *Mohawk Girls,* released in 2005. The film featured three teenagers on the Kahnawake Reserve: Lauren, Amy, and Felicia.

The character Lauren celebrated her sixteenth birthday in the film. She was attending Queen of Angels academy in Montreal, and saw the possibility of a bigger outside world, but she was appalled by the racial and ethnic divisions she felt in Kahnawake. Why, she wondered, did an American Indian woman lose her tribal status by marrying a non-Indian man? Wasn't there enough mixing among the races to show that no one was really "pure blooded?"

The character Amy was about to graduate from Kahnawake High School, and her fondest dream was that her parents— who had been divorced for many years—would agree to get

(12 hectares) of Mohawk land and because it was intended to expand in an area where Mohawk graves had been dug.

The conflict began in the spring of 1990, but it became much worse when a handful of gun-toting Warriors, flush from triumphs at Akwesasne, came north to Kanesatake. Tactics that had worked rather well on the reservation (the use of hoods and masks and the display of semi-automatic weapons) were less effective in the

along for just one day, so that it could be one of happiness. She knew great comfort in the presence of her grandparents, who had raised her, but there was a sore, empty place in her heart. Like many other Mohawk adolescents, she wondered if she was in danger of losing her traditions. Then again, some of the traditions seemed obsolete, she thought. Some Mohawk actually protested the coming of street lights to Kahnawake, saying it was not the American Indian way.

Felicia, the youngest girl in the film, was a student at the Kahnawake Survival School. Not only did students learn to "survive" in nature and in the "civilized" world, but they received Mohawk language education, and were steeped in the traditions of their tribe. Proud of her ancestors, Felicia was a fine singer who often traveled with the Kahnawake Survival School choral group. Her future seemed bright, with one major exception: She had a pigmentation problem that might well leave her blind by the age of 25. When asked how she felt about this, Felicia replied that the doctors were too pessimistic, but even if they were right, she would deal with that when the time came.

Mohawk Girls ends on a mixed note. The viewer is touched by the struggles of these adolescents, and can see resilience in them that may take them far. At the same time, the difference between the native and non-native world is highlighted, and one sees the possibility that Kahnawake and Montreal—only six miles, or 10 km apart—may never come together.

suburbs close to Montreal, where every Warrior move was shadowed by the press. There were many tense moments, but the one that was seen by millions of Canadians and other people around the world was a face-off between a ferocious-looking Warrior codenamed "Lasagna" and Canadian Private Patrick Cloutier, who looked baby-faced by comparison. Neither man was harmed.

The Warriors had miscalculated. Even as their movement won them sympathy in foreign capitals, their credibility at home sank to a low ebb. Polls showed that white Canadians were generally sympathetic concerning the golf course, but that they detested the actions taken by the Warriors.

The conflict expanded in August when the community of Kahnawake seized and held Mercier Bridge from the south side of the St. Lawrence to Montreal. Many of the Mohawk who took part in this action were former workers in high steel. They therefore knew how to handle themselves in dangerous situations. Their actions made life painfully difficult for their non-Indian neighbors, who could not commute to Montreal, and public opinion turned against the protestors. Cries of "Savages, go home!" and "We want the army!" were heard from anti-Mohawk crowds in neighboring Chauteaguay. One of the worst scenes took place when about 60 cars containing Mohawk fleeing Kahnawake were stoned by non-Indian Canadians.

The Canadian prime minister and minister of Native Affairs finally found a compromise, under which the Canadian government purchased the would-be golf course land and gave it to the Mohawk of Kanesatake. Even so, the armed stand-offs of the summer of 1990 remained in the minds of Canadians, and some Americans, for the next decade.

A NEW BEGINNING

By 1993, Mohawk Chief Tom Porter had become disillusioned by the split between the gambling and anti-gambling factions. That year he saw an opportunity to purchase 300 acres (120 ha) of land in Fonda, New York, a town settled by an ancestor of Henry Fonda, who played the leading male role in *Drums Along the Mohawk*. Porter was a nephew of Chief Standing Arrow, who made an unsuccessful attempt to occupy New York land in 1957. When the chance came to buy land in Fonda, Porter jumped at the chance. Before long he and a handful of friends established *Kanatsiohareke* ("place of the clean pot"), a traditional Mohawk community in upstate New York. The book of the same name describes the difficulties of finding a full and accurate history in the Mohawk Valley:

> A visitor to the Mohawk Valley today would have to look around deliberately to find signs of its Mohawk past. Fort Hunter, the location of a significant Mohawk village in the 1700s, has a museum—devoted to the Erie Canal. Fort Stanwix, located at the portage between the Mohawk Valley and Lake Ontario, was the place of at least two important treaties, but the restored fort focuses mainly on a two-week period during the American Revolution.

Happily, it is possible to find Mohawk history if one digs deeper.

> From Schenectady to Rome, it is almost impossible to throw a stone in the valley without hitting a place that has historical significance in Mohawk terms. Archeological sites are layered upon one another, up and down the Mohawk River.

Porter's move to the valley marked a new beginning for Mohawk people in the area. How he obtained the money to purchase the land has never been revealed. Some believe that actress Jane Fonda—a descendant of Jelles Fonda and well known for her activism on behalf of Native Americans—may have quietly given the money to Porter's group.

THE NEW MILLENNIUM

At the beginning of the new millennium, things did not look bright for the Mohawk. Whether they were on American or

This photograph shows the rich mixture of native tradition and popular culture in Mohawk communities. The flag of the Mohawk Nation is proudly displayed, while the youngest child wears a shirt that proclaims "Batman," showing how Anglo culture has filtered into traditional communities.

Canadian soil, the Mohawk people suffered from higher rates of poverty, illness, and disease than their Anglo neighbors. Worse, the reserves and reservations seemed doomed to be hold-outs against the way of life in the twenty-first century. To be sure, there were bright spots.

- More Mohawk attended institutes of higher education than ever before.
- More Mohawk had access to medical care than in the past.

These were counterbalanced by other factors:

- Canadian and American Mohawk were still separated by the boundary.
- There was little consensus about what it meant to be a Mohawk in the twenty-first century. (Was it a matter of blood, or a matter of culture and language?)

Few people had answers to these perplexing issues. Some of the great leaders of the previous generation had already passed away when they were needed most. No wise person would rule out success for the Mohawk in the new century, but circumstances suggested that it would take a mighty effort to leapfrog over the difficulties. Filmmaker Tracey Deer posed this question in her landmark *Mohawk Girls:* "Was I less Mohawk because I wanted to make it in the outside world?"

This question has been asked by many Mohawk before, including ironworkers, steelworkers, basket makers, and even circus performers. Given the inherent conflicts between native life and full participation in non-native society, it is likely that the question will continue to be posed, and that each generation of Mohawk will develop an answer appropriate to their time and place.

Chronology

1142   Possible date for the founding of the League of Five Nations.

1609   First arrival of white Europeans to the New World.

1640s to 1650s   A series of conflicts over the fur trade, called the Beaver Wars, are fought between the English and Dutch-supported Mohawk and the French-backed Algonquian.

1689   The first of the French and Indian wars, King William's War, begins. The French and their American Indian allies

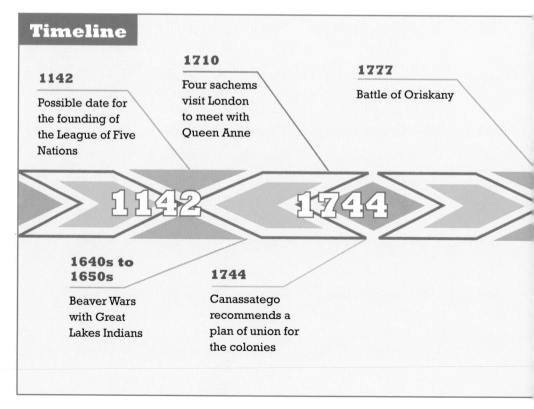

Timeline

1142

Possible date for the founding of the League of Five Nations

1710

Four sachems visit London to meet with Queen Anne

1777

Battle of Oriskany

1142   1744

1640s to 1650s

Beaver Wars with Great Lakes Indians

1744

Canassatego recommends a plan of union for the colonies

and the British and their American Indian allies fight for control of the interior of North America.

1690   In retaliation for British-supported raids by the Iroquois, French commandos and Sault and Algonquin Indians attack Schenectady, New York.

1696   King Louis XIV issues a proclamation suspending the French fur trade in the Great Lakes. Still the fighting continues, and the French invade Onondaga territory.

1697   King William's War ends with the Treaty of Ryswick. The treaty places the Iroquois under British protection, despite Iroquois' opposition. The Iroquois agree to remain neutral during any future disputes between Great Britain and France.

1702   King William dies; the second in the series of French and Indian wars, called Queen Anne's War, begins.

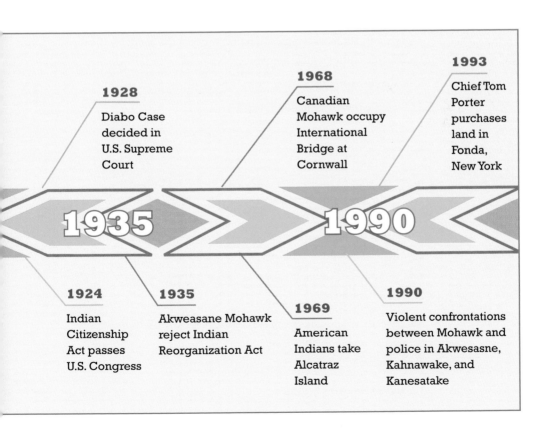

1928
Diabo Case decided in U.S. Supreme Court

1968
Canadian Mohawk occupy International Bridge at Cornwall

1993
Chief Tom Porter purchases land in Fonda, New York

1935

1990

1924
Indian Citizenship Act passes U.S. Congress

1935
Akweasane Mohawk reject Indian Reorganization Act

1969
American Indians take Alcatraz Island

1990
Violent confrontations between Mohawk and police in Akwesasne, Kahnawake, and Kanesatake

1710	As part of a diplomatic visit, four sachems visit London to meet with Queen Anne. They are received as diplomats, and visit the Tower of London and St. Paul's Cathedral, and are taken through the streets in royal carriages.
1713	The Treaty of Utrecht is signed between Great Britain and France. The Five Nations are described as subjects of Queen Anne and Great Britain.
1722	The Tuscarora join the Five Nations, making the confederacy the Six Nations.
1744	Canassatego recommends a plan of union for the colonies.
1754	Representatives of seven of the British North American colonies meet in Albany, New York, from June 19 to July 11 to discuss better relations with Native Americans. This conference, called the Albany Congress, produces Ben Franklin's Albany Plan of Union.
1755	William Johnson (British agent to the Iroquois), with his troops and Mohawk allies, attempts to expel the French during the battle of Lake George.
1759	After a 19-day siege, Fort Niagara falls to the British; the French are then defeated in Quebec.
1760	Montreal falls to the British; most of the fighting ends in the French and Indian War.
1763	The French and Indian wars officially end with the signing of the Treaty of Paris on February 10. This begins an extensive period of British dominance outside of Europe. King George issues the Royal Proclamation of 1763 on October 7, creating a boundary between British colonies on the Atlantic coast and Native lands west of the Appalachian Mountains.
1768	Treaty of Fort Stanwix is signed in Rome, New York. It is created to adjust the boundary line set forth in the Royal Proclamation.
1775	Revolutionary War begins.

1777	British Loyalists and allies from the Six Nations fight against the Patriots during the battle of Oriskany.
1784	Iroquois gives up all claims to Ohio Territory and other tracts of land in Pennsylvania in the second Treaty of Fort Stanwix.
1785	Joseph Brant establishes Six Nations Reserve in Ontario, Canada.
1795	Jay Treaty recognizes right of American Indians to cross the U.S.-Canada border freely.
1799	Seneca prophet Handsome Lake experiences visions that later play a significant role in the preservation of the Iroquois cultural heritage.
1860	Visit of Prince Albert brings increased visibility to the Canadian Mohawk.
1869	Canadian Indian Act requires families to trace descent through the father.
1900	Native American population falls to about 237,000.
1914 to 1918	Many Mohawk participate in World War I.
1924	U.S. Congress passes the Indian Citizenship Act (also known as the Snyder Act). It grants full citizenship to America's indigenous peoples.
1928	The Mohawk and Paul Diabo win major victory in the U.S. Supreme Court. He had challenged immigration laws for American Indians that crossed the Canadian border to work in the United States.
1935	Akweasane Mohawk reject Indian Reorganization Act (also known as the Wheeler-Howard Act or the Indian New Deal). It reverses the Dawes Act and restores the tribal land base, but is not successful in allowing tribes to self-govern.
1942	A group of Six Nations chiefs declare war on Axis powers in World War II

1968	Canadian Mohawk occupy International Bridge at Cornwall.
1969	American Indians occupy Alcatraz Island.
1978	Kahnawake Survival School established.
1980	Jay Silverheels, who plays Lone Ranger's sidekick, Tonto, dies.
1985	Canadian law regarding patrilineal descent changes.
1988	Casinos allowed on Native American reservations.
1989	Tensions build over casinos in Akwesasane.
1990	Violent confrontations between Mohawk and police in Akwesasne, Kahnawake, and Kanesatake.
1990	*Dances with Wolves* released.
1991	*Last of the Mohicans* released.
1993	Chief Tom Porter purchases land in Fonda, New York.

Glossary

Akwesasne In Mohawk (Kanien'keha) language, *Akwesasne* means "Land Where the Partridge Drums." It began as one of the smallest Mohawk communities on the St. Lawrence River and is now the largest population and land area of the Kanien'keha:ka community, with 12,000 residents.

Akwesasne Notes A news journal established in 1969 to report on issues and concerns of Native Americans. It is known as the "Voice of Indigenous Peoples."

Alcatraz Island This small island in California's San Francisco Bay first served as a lighthouse, then a military fort, a military prison, and finally and most famously as a federal prison until 1963. In 1969 a group of Native Americans from different tribes occupied the island and claimed it as reparations, or payment, for broken treaties.

Cohoes Falls Located on the Mohawk River in New York State and originally called Ga-ha-oose ("The Place of the Falling Canoe"), the falls is the site where the Great Peacemaker, Deganawida, performed a feat of supernatural strength. This convinced the Mohawk to become the founders of the Iroquois Confederacy.

Condolence ceremony The act of repairing physical and psychological damages so that one can hear properly, see properly, and think properly in a council fire.

Council Fire The central decision-making place in Six Nations life; prior to 1777, it was always at Onondaga, near present-day Syracuse, New York.

Dawes Allotment Act Enacted in 1887, this act distributed tribally held land into individually owned parcels and opened surplus land to non-Indians.

Five Nations The original Iroquois League, or Confederacy, it comprised the Mohawk, Oneida, Onondaga, Cayuga, Seneca tribes.

Johnson Hall Located in present-day Johnstown, New York, it was the home of Sir William Johnson, New York's agent to the Iroquois. Johnson Hall was a major site for council fires in the 1760s and 1770s.

Kahnawake Mohawk Territory   Meaning "By the Rapids," this Mohawk reserve on the south side of the St. Lawrence River in Quebec is one of several Kanien'keha:ka territories of the Mohawk within the Canadian border.

Kanatsiohareke   This word means "Place of the Clean Pot." It is a traditional Mohawk settlement in Fonda, New York, built in 1993 by Chief Tom Porter.

Mohawk River   A glacially carved 140-mile (230-km) river in New York State that runs from the Adirondacks to its confluence with the Hudson River. Throughout history, it served as an important transportation link to the west through the Appalachian Mountains, and was the site of many important battles including the French and Indian War and the American Revolutionary War.

Mohawk River Valley   The land on either side of the Mohawk River, famed for the fertility of its soil and the beauty of its surroundings.

Mohawk Warriors   Founded in the 1970s, this militant Kanesatake group was involved in a land dispute (starting July 11, 1990) over Oka, Quebec's plans to develop a golf course on sacred Mohawk ground. The local Mohawks were joined in their protest by other Native Americans from across Canada and the United States. After 78 days and many confrontations with Canadian military and police, the golf course plan was cancelled.

Niagara Falls   This waterfall marked the western boundary of the Five Nations in the seventeenth and eighteenth centuries.

Sachem   A chief of the ruling council of the Iroquois Confederacy.

Six Nations   The original people of the Iroquois Confederacy, along with the Tuscarora, who joined in 1722. Benjamin Franklin and Thomas Jefferson drew from this confederacy to create the tenets of the United States democracy.

Termination Policy   A U.S. federal policy from the mid-1940s to the mid-1960s in which the government attempted to assimilate Native Americans into "mainstream" American society. Native Americans were granted the rights and privileges of American citizenship while terminating their rights to land, hunting, and fishing; federal support for healthcare and education programs; resources for police and fire departments on reservations; and individual tribes' recognition as sovereign dependent nations.

Bibliography

Akwesasne Notes. *Basic Call to Consciousness*. Rooseveltoron, N.Y.: Akwesasne Notes, 1978.

Bond, Richmond P. *Queen Anne's American Kings*. Oxford, UK: The Clarendon Press, 1952.

Deer, Tracey. *Mohawk Girls* (film). National Film Board of Canada, 2005.

Blanchard, David S. "Patterns of Tradition and Change: The re-creation of Iroquois Culture at Kanhawke." Unpublished dissertation for the University of Chicago, 1981.

Colden, Cadwallader. *The History of the Five Indian Nations, depending on the Province of New York in America*. Ithaca, N.Y.: Cornell University Press, 1964.

Costner, Kevin. *Dances with Wolves* (film). Paramount Pictures, 1990.

Ford, John. *Drums Along the Mohawk* (film). 20th Century Fox, 1939.

George-Kanentiio, Douglas M. *Iroquois on Fire: A Voice from the Mohawk Nation*. Lincoln: University of Nebraska Press, 2008.

Hauptman, Laurence M. *Seven Generations of Iroquois Leadership: The Six Nations Since 1800*. Syracuse, N.Y.: Syracuse University Press, 2008.

Hauptman, Laurence M. *The Iroquois and the New Deal*. Syracuse, N.Y.: Syracuse University Press, 1981.

"Jay Silverheels, Actor, 62, Dead; Was Tonto in TV 'Lone Ranger.'" *New York Times*, March 6, 1980, D:19.

Johansen, Bruce E. *Life and Death in Mohawk Country*. Golden, Colo.: North American Press, 1993.

Mann, Michael. *Last of the Mohicans* (film). 20th Century Fox, 1991.

O'Callaghan, E.B., ed. *Documentary History of the State of New York*. 4 Vols. Albany, N.Y.: Weed, Parsons, & Co, 1849.

Ransen, Mort. *You Are on Indian Land* (film). Film Board of Canada, 1969.

Shannon, Timothy J. *Indians and Colonists at the Crossroads of Empire: The Albany Congress of 1754*. Ithaca, N.Y.: Cornell University Press, 2000.

Sivertsen, Barbara J. *Turtles, Wolves, and Bears: A Mohawk Family History*. Bowie, Md.: Heritage Books, 1996.

Venables, Robert W., ed. *The Six Nations of New York: The 1892 United States Extra Census Bulletin.* Ithaca, N.Y.: Cornell University Press, 1995.

Vesilind, Pritt J., and Sarah Leen. "Common ground, different dreams: the U.S.-Canada border." *National Geographic,* February 1990, pp. 94–127.

Further Resources

Borneman, Walter R. *The French and Indian War: Deciding the Fate of North America.* New York: HarperPerennial, 2007.

O'Connor, George. *Journey into Mohawk Country.* New York: First Second, 2006.

Porter, Tom. *Kanatsiohareke: Traditional Mohawk Indians Return to their Ancestral Homeland.* Greenfield Center, N.Y.: Bowman Books, 2006.

Shorto, Russell. *Island at the Center of the World: The Epic Story of Dutch Manhattan and the Forgotten Colony that Shaped America.* New York: Vintage, 2005.

Slapin, Beverly and Doris Seale, editors. *Through Indian Eyes: The Native Experience in Books for Children.* Los Angeles: American Indian Studies Center, 1998.

Web sites

Akwesasne Cultural Center

http://www.akwesasneculture.org/

This nonprofit organization was developed to increase awareness of Mohawk culture and history. They have collected audiotapes, posters, books, and videos and assembled them into kits for schools and other organizations.

Mohawk Nation Council of Chiefs

http://www.mohawknation.org/

The official site for the Mohawk Nation Council of Chiefs, the national government of the Kanien'keha:ka people.

Mohawk Nation News

http://www.mohawknationnews.com/

This is the site for the internationally recognized news service, Mohawk Nation News. It provides articles and commentary on legal issues, culture, history, and current news that affect the nation.

Mohawk Tribe

http://www.mohawktribe.com/

This site is a resource for people that seek information about the Mohawk tribe and Iroquois League. It includes historical documents, biographies, definitions for cultural symbols, and a discussion board.

Noteworthy Indian Museum

http://www.greatturtle.net/aboutus.html

An online visit to the museum that features baskets, clay pots, and other artifacts from the beginnings of the Mohawk nation.

Smithsonian National Museum of the American Indian

http://www.nmai.si.edu/

This museum, which is the sixteenth museum of the Smithsonian Institution, is the first national museum dedicated to the preservation, study, and exhibition of the culture of Native Americans.

Picture Credits

YYYYYYYYYYYYYYYYYYYY

PAGE:

16:     © Infobase Publishing

21:     SSPL/Science Museum / Art Resource, NY

26:     © North Wind Picture Archives / Alamy

28:     © Infobase Publishing

31:     Wampum Belt, American Iroquoian or Algonquian tribe, possible 17th century, (shell beads and 'Indian' hemp), / © Ashmolean Museum, University of Oxford, UK / The Bridgeman Art Library

35:     North Wind Picture Archives via AP Images

41:     ac Yec Neen Ho Gar Ton, Emperor of the Six Nations, 1710 (oil on canvas), Verelst, Johannes or Jan (b.1648–fl.1719) / Private Collection / The Bridgeman Art Library

41:     King of the River Nations, 1710 (oil on canvas), Verelst, Johannes or Jan (b.1648–fl.1719) / Private Collection / The Bridgeman Art Library

47:     Courtesy of the Library of Congress, LC-USZ62-2695 (b&w film copy neg.). Digital ID 3a06347

51:     John Fadden

55:     Science & Society Picture Library/Getty Images

60:     The Shooting of General Braddock at Fort Duquesne, Pittsburgh, 1755 (oil on canvas), Deming, Edwin Willard (1860–1942) / State Historical Society of Wisconsin, Madison, USA / The Bridgeman Art Library

62:     North Wind Picture Archives via AP Images

66:     Joseph Brant, Chief of the Mohawks, 1742–1807, Romney, George (1734–1802) / National Gallery of Canada, Ottawa, Ontario, Canada / The Bridgeman Art Library

72:     © Infobase Publishing

76:     © Bettmann/CORBIS

80:     Courtesy of the Library of Congress, reproduction #LC-USZ62-132279 (b&w film copy neg.) DIGITAL ID: (b&w film copy neg.) cph 3c32279

85:     Courtesy of the Library of Congress LC-USZ62-132280 (b&w film copy neg.) DIGITAL ID: (b&w film copy neg.) cph 3c32280

89:     © CORBIS

95:	AP Images
98:	ABC/Photofest
101:	AP Images
110:	© Christopher J. Morris/Corbis
116:	© Megapress / Alamy

Index

About the Contributors

Author **SAMUEL WILLARD CROMPTON** lives in Massachusetts, 20 miles south of the Mohawk Trail, which is noted for being the invasion route Mohawk warriors used in the seventeenth and eighteenth centuries. Like many white Americans, he has family stories of American Indian blood in the family; like most, he had been unable to confirm them. Crompton teaches history at Holyoke Community College, in his native Massachusetts. He is the editor of the *Illustrated Atlas of Native American History,* published in 1999.

Series editor **PAUL C. ROSIER** received his Ph.D. in American History from the University of Rochester in 1998. Dr. Rosier currently serves as Associate Professor of History at Villanova University (Villanova, Pennsylvania), where he teaches Native American History, American Environmental History, Global Environmental Justice Movements, History of American Capitalism, and World History.

In 2001 the University of Nebraska Press published his first book, *Rebirth of the Blackfeet Nation, 1912–1954;* in 2003, Greenwood Press published *Native American Issues* as part of its Contemporary Ethnic American Issues series. In 2006 he co-edited an international volume called *Echoes from the Poisoned Well: Global Memories of Environmental Injustice.* Dr. Rosier has also published articles in the *American Indian Culture and Research Journal,* the *Journal of American Ethnic History,* and *The Journal of American History.* His *Journal of American History* article, entitled "'They Are Ancestral Homelands: Race, Place, and Politics in Cold War Native America, 1945–1961," was selected for inclusion in *The Ten Best History Essays of 2006–2007,* published by Palgrave MacMillan in 2008; and it won the Western History Association's 2007 Arrell Gibson Award for Best Essay on the history of Native Americans. In 2009 Harvard University Press published his latest book, *Serving Their Country: American Indian Politics and Patriotism in the Twentieth Century.*